Your Child Is
SMARTER
Than You Think!

"What she says is so practical. When I go to her seminars, I know I can take what she says home with me and use it in my everyday life."

—**Tracy McCoy**, Mother

"She is radiantly enthusiastic about her work with children and parents."

—**Dorothy Hammert**, Grandmother

"Dr. Draper is as down-to-earth as the sod dugout my mother lived in, and as far reaching as the space capsule I traveled in."

—**Lt. Gen. Thomas P. Stafford** USAF (Ret.), Astronaut

"If I could be anything in the world, I would be a flower in Wanda's garden because I know that she would take good care of me."

—**Austin Vanderlyn**, age 8

Your Child Is SMARTER
Than You Think!

Unleashing Your Child's UNLIMITED *Potential*

WANDA DRAPER

NEW YORK

Your Child Is SMARTER Than You Think!
Unleashing Your Child's UNLIMITED *Potential*

© 2014 WANDA DRAPER.

Published in New York, New York, by Morgan James Publishing. Morgan James and The Entrepreneurial Publisher are trademarks of Morgan James, LLC. www.MorganJamesPublishing.com

The Morgan James Speakers Group can bring authors to your live event. For more information or to book an event visit The Morgan James Speakers Group at www.TheMorganJamesSpeakersGroup.com.

FREE eBook edition for your
existing eReader with purchase

_____

PRINT NAME ABOVE

For more information,
instructions, restrictions, and
to register your copy, go to
www.bitlit.ca/readers/register
or use your QR Reader to scan
the barcode:

ISBN 978-1-61448-766-1 paperback
ISBN 978-1-61448-767-8 eBook
ISBN 978-1-61448-768-5 audio
ISBN 978-1-61448-991-7 hardcover
Library of Congress Control Number:
2013951451

Cover Design by:
Rachel Lopez
www.r2cdesign.com

Interior Design by:
Bonnie Bushman
bonnie@caboodlegraphics.com

In an effort to support local communities, raise awareness and funds, Morgan James Publishing donates a percentage of all book sales for the life of each book to Habitat for Humanity Peninsula and Greater Williamsburg.

Get involved today, visit
www.MorganJamesBuilds.com

Habitat
for Humanity®
Peninsula and
Greater Williamsburg
Building Partner

To Maya and Valerie
For their years of friendship and encouragement

Contents

Foreword

The world is becoming smaller, yet the problems of daily living are becoming greater. We are constantly bombarded by dramatic changes and unexpected crises. Parents are caught in the dilemma of managing to give their children the right start in life while meeting their own personal and family needs.

Wanda Draper illustrates the relationship of how children learn and how they behave. She gives practical suggestions for how parents can enhance their children's potential for success in school by establishing trust and mutual relationships during the first few years of life.

<u>Your Child is Smarter than You Think!</u> is one of the most sensible, inspiring, and down-to-earth books on how to be a successful parent while unleashing your child's unlimited potential. Wanda Draper has an extraordinary gift for communicating with parents and teachers about ideas that work. Her practical teachings grow out of three decades of direct experience with children of all ages, including those with special needs, multi-racial and multi-cultural endowments.

She is a highly respected authority in the field of child development. Dr. Draper is Professor Emeritus of Psychiatry and Behavior Sciences in the College of Medicine, University of Oklahoma where she taught for twenty years. Her books have been used across the US and in other countries, including in her seminars in Hong Kong, Singapore, and Romania, and in teaching residents in medical school in Bucharest. She led teams of US professionals in their work with doctors and nurses in Romanian orphanages. Her work as a consultant for twenty-five years with Head Start teachers grew out of her interest in parent-child relationships.

In her studies of super achievers, Dr. Draper interviewed Russian, Czech, and Romanian cosmonauts, and American astronauts in addition to high school students in the renowned Oklahoma School of Science and Mathematics. Her developmental seminars for psychiatry residents, accompanied by on-the-floor experiences with healthy children, provided a sound basis for the study of pathology and developmental disorders. As co-director of the diagnostic and therapeutic center for special needs children, she supervised psychiatry and pediatric residents, physical therapy and nursing students, and nanny interns. Her classes in behavioral sciences for medical students sparked a realistic view of spiraling development from infancy through adolescence, especially when she brought young children into the classroom to play in order to illustrate their varying levels of intellectual and social abilities.

Wanda's early career of teaching students from preschool to college, inspired her to write textbooks. Then she developed handbooks, audio and video materials for students and adults. As a result of her vast experience in the field of human development, her career has evolved into consulting for capital court cases. While working on over one hundred capital murder cases, she has seen first hand, the impact of childhood problems and the relationship between what happens in the early years of development and adult outcomes. Her publications are designed to help parents succeed in the awesome task of guiding their children's behavior and making way for unlimited possibilities as they learn to express their feelings and thoughts while they develop caring attitudes, build self confidence, get along with others, and practice responsible behavior. I've known Wanda Draper and her work for over thirty years and I am pleased to say that **Your Child is Smarter than You Think!** is worth its weight in gold.

Lt. General Thomas P. Stafford, USAF (Ret.) Astronaut
Pilot Gemini VI
Cdr. Gemini IX
Cdr. Apollo X
Cdr. Apollo-Soyuz
USAF Deputy-Chief of Staff for R&D

Acknowledgments

I am especially grateful to Sarah-Nicole Partin for her help in preparing the manuscript, and for her expertise in managing the computer technology. Her critique and suggestions, together with her never-ending enthusiasm, have added a stimulating dimension to this endeavor.

Dr. Howard Gardner, psychologist and professor of neuroscience, cognition, and education at Harvard University, has made landmark contributions to how we view human intelligence. I am especially grateful for Dr. Gardner's groundbreaking work on his theory of multiple intelligences and its profound influence on my thinking about how children learn.

To Terry Whalin, my acquisitions editor at Morgan James, I give special thanks for his interest and encouragement in pursuing this writing project, and to Hank Frazee for believing in the merits of the manuscript.

My appreciation cannot be overstated for the Oklahoma School of Science and Mathematics, where for seven years I worked closely with high school juniors and seniors. The students in this public school come from a wide range of economic and ethnic backgrounds, and they convinced me by their behavior and performance that academic success is imminent when students experience a learning atmosphere in which parents and teachers genuinely care about them and their progress. A typical course load for these students includes: calculus, physics, computer science, biology, anatomy, chemistry, history, English, foreign language, and behavioral science. Obviously, these students have no time to waste. They are motivated to study and perform because the school expects it, and their parents and peers expect it. The dropout rate is practically nonexistent. Another factor that contributes to the success of these students is that parents and the school share the same philosophy about the school's purpose and about what students are capable of achieving.

I give special thanks to Courtney Crawford and all those who expressed personal thoughts and feelings in their writings.

I should like to acknowledge the many parents and teachers, and their children and students, without whom this book would have little meaning. For the experiences we shared taught me that development of mind, body, and spirit evolves on a very practical and down-to-earth pathway of personal learning.

Introduction

America is blessed with smart children. They are not dumb, they are not slow, and they are not lazy. Some lack opportunity, but they rarely lack potential. I would argue that there is no shortage of intelligence—only shortage of actualizing it. Furthermore, I would estimate that of all children in America, about 90 percent are capable of making A's and B's. Yet current reports indicate that only about 10 percent reflect world-class scholarship.

Your child has more brainpower than any computer or technological device known to humanity. Consider these facts about your child's mental capacity: at birth the human brain weighs about 350 grams, and by the age of 14 or 15 years, it has increased to about 1,450 grams. This enormous expansion of brain matter carries with it the power to go beyond the limits expressed in grades, IQ, or achievement test scores.

Learning occurs when one is motivated. Without motivation, little more than memorization and short-term recall occurs, and even that may be reduced. Motivation is directly impacted by one's emotional state—how one feels. These feelings usually center on oneself and the ideas as they exist in the mind of the individual.

What we expect from our children is often what we get. When we stop catering to special interest groups who want to lower the reading levels, students will feel better about their own minds. Students are not naïve; they quickly sense what others think about them. They are capable of reaching for and mastering vocabularies and reading comprehension when the subject matter is represented in an exciting and alluring manner. When we project the illusion that high school seniors can only read at an eighth grade level, we are violating the integrity of their very beings and bestowing upon them the right to fail.

I suggest that neither the reading levels of textbooks, nor the duration of the school year, have as much impact on helping children learn as does the classroom's emotional and learning atmosphere and the teacher-student relationships. Students will generally follow the lead of the teacher—go slow and they'll do the same; go fast and they'll keep up. I would estimate that in most schools what is covered in a nine-month period of classroom time could be condensed into about three to six months.

I am privileged to have worked as a teacher for twenty years from preschool through high school and college, and for another twenty years in a college of medicine teaching psychiatry residents. The students taught me how to teach. My first year of teaching was with sixth graders in a low-income community. I learned firsthand that humans have a natural need to know and that learning is its own reward. These children taught me how students learn, how they feel about themselves, and how they perceive life.

In my study of super achievers, I interviewed astronauts and cosmonauts, as well as high school students. I discovered five factors necessary for a person to succeed in school and in life: **self-confidence, getting along with others, vision or a sense of wonder, focus,** and **self-reflection.** These qualities don't have to be taught directly; they emerge naturally in students whose parents, teachers, and administrators model them in everyday life.

Parents who hold a broad view of possibilities extend to their children the idea of lots of options by which to solve problems and make headway. Those who consistently show a genuine interest in their children's ideas and opinions—engaging them in expressing what they think—help them build self-confidence. Getting along with others is a natural outcome when children are treated with respect and dignity by their parents and teachers, and when they see respect for others exemplified around them. A sense of wonder expands one's vision and brings about an expanded view of oneself and the world. When we guide children in developing habits of focus and concentration, until the task is complete, we will see positive results. Self-reflection is a behavior that every student engages in, whether overtly or covertly, when a test paper is returned or when feedback or a grade is received. How open students are to self-evaluation depends greatly on how parents and teachers respond to them. Children are smart, and they find ways to protect their own dignity, even if it means fabricating test results or losing grade reports.

Educating our children comes down to the practical application of how children think and learn in relation to how they feel. From infancy through adolescence, children are whole human beings, and they carry with them their unique talents and abilities, along with their emotional baggage. Whether in grade school or high school, when students manifest an attachment to learning, a *bond between feeling and intellect* will drive them to success. Feelings provide the energy source that powers the vehicle of intellect, and *perception guides the way*.

So often when parents come to me with concerns about their children, especially involving their behavior, my response is, "That's because your child is smarter than you think!" I have written this book with the thought of sharing some of what I have gleaned from working with parents, teachers, and children of all ages. The goal of this writing is fourfold: (1) to increase awareness of a child's capabilities and potential, (2) to better understand and accept the feelings and thoughts of a child, (3) to appreciate the child's perception, and (4) to act in relation to what will bring about a stronger and more meaningful connection between you and your child or your student.

CHAPTER 1

Essentials for Success

Your child has the capacity to succeed—in life and in school. I believe that every child is endowed with sensitivity, or a spirit of hope from within, that makes it possible to adapt to virtually any situation. While each child portrays a unique range of feelings and social inclinations, and breadth of intelligence, so does each have the capacity to manifest his or her own potential.

When a child is born, 350 grams of brain matter contains the brainpower that has the potential to unleash dynamic possibilities. By the middle of a child's fourteenth year of life, brain matter has increased to 1,450 grams, expanding brainpower potential. Except for those with a brain injury, a disease, or neurological damage, all children have about the same brain capacity.

Why, then, aren't all children reflecting their abilities and their talents? And why are some children making top grades when they seem to be working against all odds? My belief is that most children live up to the images they create of themselves. Those who see themselves as smart will make every effort to uphold that image.

Each child comes into the world with a particular set of hereditary characteristics, and into a range of family and environmental circumstances. As the child develops, he or she gradually creates a perception of self. This perception, or belief, about oneself is formed primarily by how the child interprets the behavior and responses of others. Right or wrong, these interpretations may be more powerful in guiding the child than any other factor. How the child sees himself or herself in light of genetic traits, life circumstances, and others' views becomes "reality" and tends to shape the patterns that govern behavior. Of course, one's views can change, so there is always hope for a better future.

Children tend to pursue what they do best. But best by what standards? A letter that I received from the father of a ten-year-old helps to make the point that a child's view of himself often is influenced by those he considered important. Here are portions of the letter from Tommy's dad:

> As you know, I have been very concerned about Tommy's grades for the last few years. A low C average gave me great concern. In my actions, intended to help, I was always trying to fix the problems that Tommy has faced, even though I was over a thousand miles away. Every time I visited him, I met with teachers, I reviewed his papers, and I let the school know I was a concerned parent.
>
> I started examining my view of Tommy and realized that I was trying to fix his grades for him because I didn't believe deep inside that he had the capacity to do it himself. I felt he had average intelligence, at best. When you told me you thought Tommy was very bright, I was relieved, yet it left me confused. *How come his grades aren't better, then?* I thought. I started looking for a way to shift my view of Tommy, and I realized that going into the fifth grade, he was also going into his fourth school. His home life was fairly unsettled. I began to see him in a different way.
>
> The next time I spoke to him, I said, "I just want you to know how proud I am of your grades." His reply was a guarded, "What?" I explained that I thought he had done well considering all the

moves and family circumstances. His response was an enthusiastic, "I'll do even better this year, Dad!" And indeed he has. I know now that Tommy can do it on his own. Naturally, I'll always be there with love and encouragement, and help if he asks for it, but I don't have to worry about fixing it. Tommy can fix it.

Success in school and in life is rooted in the love and trust that grow out of early relationships between parents and their children. The kind of personal interchanges that form in the early months and years set the stage for how children will perform later. As they interact with others, they begin to form images of themselves that ultimately lead to success or failure.

One's self-image is framed within everyday experiences. What happens to a child each day gradually accumulates until a snowball effect collects enough information to form a picture that the child believes is real. This mental picture may be fairly accurate, or it may be distorted, depending on how the child interprets the actions of others. For example, a child who is ignored a lot, except when misbehaving, soon views herself as important mainly when she's in trouble. She will do what she has to in order to live up to this image. Every child wants to feel important, even if it has to be for the wrong reasons.

In order to change one's self-image, the experiences that help form that image also must change. Even a child who misbehaves to get attention likely will develop new patterns of behavior if she begins to get positive feedback when she behaves appropriately.

We had a child in our kindergarten several years ago who continually challenged the teacher with his devious and unpredictable misdeeds. He caused so much disruption that she could hardly give proper attention to the other children. One day she came to me and said that she had tried everything and nothing seemed to work—he had just pulled down a curtain with his teeth. Somewhat out of desperation, I said to her: "From now on, stop using his name when he does anything inappropriate. Only use his name when his behavior is acceptable. Let's try separating his identity from misbehavior, and maybe we can help him change his self-image."

After only four days, the teacher came to me and reported that he had turned his behavior around completely. He even approached her and asked, "Why are you doing that to me?" She replied, "Doing what?" He said, "You know, doing *that* to me." While he could not explain what was happening, he knew it was different. He felt different. He felt affirmed for good behavior. The avoidance of using his name in connection with misbehavior helped him to reframe his self-image. While he never understood the process, the results were dramatic. He became a delightful child who loved the teacher—and himself.

The responses that we give to children have such powerful influence on them. It's as though they are viewing themselves in magical mirrors, forming reflections from the feedback that lets them know how they are doing. And while their images will change over time, their framing is secured by the strength of love and encouragement from those who are there for them. Success will be the natural outcome for those children who strive to live up to positive images of themselves.

Some children seem to be self-motivated. They set high standards regardless of those around them. Most, however, have such a natural desire to belong that they do whatever it takes to prove that the parents' views are correct, or that teachers' notions about them are valid. They tend to live out what they interpret to be the perceptions of those around them.

Furthermore, every child is endowed with the ability to perceive the world either as a friendly place, filled with joy and opportunity, or as a threatening place, filled with fear and deprivation. The child's view of the world will greatly determine which path in life to pursue.

In my work, with more than one hundred defendants charged with capital murder, about 95 percent of them viewed the world as a fearful and threatening place. This view was not difficult for me to understand after I interviewed family members, teachers, and others who shed light on the defendants' growing-up experiences.

Families, schools, and communities that reflect the world as a friendly place provide the first step in helping children to develop five essential qualities that contribute to success in school and in life:

- Getting along with others
- Self-confidence
- Vision and a sense of wonder
- The ability to focus
- Self-reflection

The more I learn from working with children and talking with parents and teachers, the stronger I feel that success in school and in life depends on the mastery of these essential qualities. And as I work with the courts on criminal cases, I see potential that has been stifled because these qualities were not accomplished during the early and adolescent school years.

In doing research on super achievers, I interviewed American astronauts and Russian, Romanian, and Czech cosmonauts. They confirmed the notion that to be successful, one must master these five qualities. When they traveled in space, they transcended their differences in cultures, ideologies, and languages because they viewed the world, literally, as "a fragile planet" in the vast universe. I was privileged to attend one of their international conferences for people who travel in space. It was quite obvious that they all got along with one another. They said that in the space program, there is an unspoken imperative that these five qualities must be mastered and maintained.

Getting Along with Others

Children who get along with others are headed for success. Those who are friendly and caring will easily attract others and make friends. As the saying goes, "The way to have a friend is to be a friend." Some children seem to have a natural tendency to be outgoing and friendly, while others have to work at it. In either case, children are smart enough to know whether or not others like or accept them. In fact, that's one of the greatest problems that plague children. They want to belong and to feel important to those around them.

Children who get along with others generally reflect the following characteristics:

- Trust in oneself and others
- The ability to share and form mutual relationships
- Skills for communicating
- A working toward common goals with others
- Enjoyment of attachments and friendships
- Affectionate and sincere relationships
- Caring attitudes

Communicating Begins with Infancy

From the first day onward, parents set the stage for sending and receiving messages between the parent and the child. *Attachment* and *bonding* begin with eye contact while they feed, hold and cuddle, and play with their baby.

Getting Along Means Communicating

The *voice* of the parent connects with the baby's mind to bring comfort and familiarity. Research indicates that babies can hear by the fifth month of prenatal development. They develop brain patterns for speech and for their native languages during the first six months of life—long before they can say a word.

Babies are quick to sense their parents' voices. Some fathers report talking to their babies several months before they are born. Later, these newborns seem to be comforted and "tuned in" to their fathers' voices.

Parents are sometimes unaware of just how much they are communicating with their young children. Toddlers who aren't talking yet hear not only what is said around them, but they hear mechanical and electronic sounds as well. Most thirteen- to sixteen-month-olds can imitate sounds of blenders, vacuum cleaners, airplanes, and more. They are able to store what they hear and imitate these sounds later. First, they just make sounds, and later, they use words. Generally, children first imitate the words they learn by being around their parents. Then, they imitate siblings and adults who take care of them.

Getting along is something that children learn best by being with others who set good examples. Talking with children opens the way for them to express their concerns and their feelings as well as their ideas. Parents and teachers serve as examples of how to talk and how to listen while interacting with children. Establishing and enforcing guidelines and limits for behavior helps children feel safe as they tread new pathways to learning.

Children who experience a sense of belonging and importance feel free to express themselves and share their ideas. On the other hand, those who hold their feelings inside may build resentment and fears of rejection regarding family members and friends. Sooner or later, children give way to their feelings and may have outbursts of temper or aggression toward others.

Children communicate in a variety of ways. Some talk a lot and listen to what others say. Some pay more attention to what they see going on around them. Still others respond to body language rather than words.

Five-year-old Allen and his mom went for their visit to the psychologist because Allen seemed to be very unhappy. Yet he kept telling his mom, "I love you, Mom. Please stay home with me. I don't want to go to school." While Allen played in the children's room, his mother met with the psychologist, who told her that Allen's problem was that he seemed unsure about his mother's love for him. So, as they were leaving, Allen's mom said to him, "Allen, you know that I love you. I will always love you." Allen looked up at her and said, "Then why don't you tell me with your eyes?"

Communication Skills Lead to Responsible Behavior

Effective communication makes way for responsible behavior. This includes sending and receiving messages in ways that have meaning for those involved. There are several ways to communicate, such as speech, body gestures, facial expressions, sign language, and voice tone.

The key to communicating:

Keep the messages simple and the channels open. For example, when a teenager is upset, there is little chance of getting a message through. Say what you mean in an honest, straightforward, and respectful way, and then stop. Too much talking may clog the process and turn the teenager off. Keep in mind that the teenager wants to get a message to you, too. Be a genuine listener.

Trust and mutual respect are forerunners to effective communication. When children trust their parents and other adults, they feel comfortable about sharing ideas and feelings. They are able to express themselves without fear of making mistakes or being ridiculed.

Get on the child's level. Interact face-to-face in a comfortable manner. This eliminates fear or threat of the adult towering over the child. Use words and sentences that the child can understand. Even before children can talk, they often grasp the idea of what you are saying.

Remain calm and confident. Whether toddler or teenager, acknowledge the importance of the child's message—even when you disagree. Avoid sudden outbursts of temper, such as shouting or hitting. Set the example you want your child or student to follow.

Listen to the child's point of view. Give the child an opportunity to express feelings and viewpoints, even when you disagree. Consider the situation from the child's position.

Treat each other with dignity. Children need to know their words have value. Both adults and children must feel respected. Stop the conversation when a child is disrespectful. Refuse to get caught up in "verbal warfare."

Make a statement of understanding before approaching a problem. This helps children know you care about their feelings. A statement such as, "I'm sure I would feel the same way if I were in your place" shows the child that you appreciate his perspective of the situation.

Acknowledge what happened. Be frank and honest. For example, "You stomped out when you could not have your way."

Direct your comments at the child's efforts or behavior. Express feelings without putting the child on the defensive. Avoid attacking the child's character. For example, "I want to talk with you about what happened. I want us to settle this problem. Even though I am angry about what you did, I care about you, and I'll do what I can to help."

Practice communication skills. Children and adults who play together open the way for sharing ideas and feelings. Since play is voluntary, there is no particular agenda and no fear or threat of punishment. Playing is a way to practice social skills that establish patterns for solving more serious problems later.

Getting along is usually more successful when children can "break out" as well as "fit in." When a child seems irritable or aggressive toward others, provide a setting that allows the child to seek solitude and be alone for a while. Looking at books, listening to music, or simply daydreaming helps a child relax. However, too much time alone may be a signal that a child needs help. Keeping open communication helps a child feel comfortable about talking when something goes wrong.

Children who are able to appropriately express themselves and get along with others are headed for success.

Self-Confidence

Self-confidence is a strong sense of feeling and knowing "I can do it." The level of this type of confidence is based on how a person perceives what he or she is doing, or what he or she can do. Self-confidence includes one's self-image and self-esteem, or self-worth. Children with self-confidence generally reflect the following characteristics:

- **A self-perception** that reflects feelings and thoughts about oneself as important and acceptable
- **A self-image** that reflects a positive view of oneself
- **Self-esteem** that reflects personal worth and confidence
- **Motivation** to act and to complete tasks
- **Trust** in one's own abilities
- **A willingness** to take risks and get involved

The building blocks for self-confidence are the skills for living and learning. These skills, beginning in childhood and continuing through adulthood, include such abilities as:

- Communication and language skills
- Thinking and problem-solving skills
- Social skills
- Emotional stability
- Physical well-being
- Creative expression

The manner in which parents and teachers treat children leaves impressions on their minds. These impressions influence a child to feel either adequate or inadequate. Children are always comparing themselves to other children and to their parents, even when others don't. They evaluate, or measure, their own sense of value by how they believe others view them.

One of the best avenues to developing self-confidence is mastery of skills that help a child know and feel that "I can." When a child has the attitude that "I can succeed," we can be sure that success is imminent. This is especially true when children have emotional support from parents and academic support from teachers.

Why do so many children say, "I can't"? Even the smartest children make this statement. There are many reasons. Children may say, "I can't" because they have needs or fears, such as:

- A need for attention
- A need to have you close and helping
- A fear of not doing it "right"
- A fear of failure
- A fear of not pleasing a parent or teacher
- Reservations about taking a risk
- A lack of trust in their own abilities

How can we help? What is the most effective response to a child who says, "I can't"? And what can adults do to help children gain the self-confidence they need to take action and push beyond the risk they may be feeling?

Many adults say, "Oh, yes, you can. I know you can." Such a response is very threatening to a child. The underlying, or psychological, message that the child may sense is, "There must be something wrong with me" or "I'm not good enough" or "I must be dumb."

Instead, simply say, "Oh, so you can't?" First of all, this is not what the child expects to hear. Second, you need to get the child to listen to what you have to say. So follow by saying something like: "It's okay if you can't. You are still learning. That's why you are in this family. I am your parent, and I will help you. Soon you will be able to do it." Or, "That's why you are in school. School is a place to practice and learn, and that's why you have teachers to help you."

Another effective response is to say, "So you can't. Perhaps we can talk about how you feel. I am interested in what you are thinking or wishing." Many children will then say, "Oh, yes, I can do it."

When a child says, "I can do it," this is an empowering statement. These words activate the child's energy and direct the child's efforts toward succeeding. But these words cannot be forced. Children do best when they think and feel they have the ability or are willing to take the risk and face the challenge.

Build on Success

Self-confidence grows as children build on their successes. The foundation begins at birth and gradually builds as successful experiences accumulate. Success is built on balancing trust and risk. Trust has its roots in:

- Love and affection
- Attachment (to parents, teachers, and friends)
- Mutual respect (for self and others)
- A strong sense of responsibility
- Images of possibilities
- Risk is usually composed of perceptions, such as:
- Excitement about the challenge
- Anxiety or worry about succeeding or failing
- A fear of loss, failure, rejection, humiliation, and the unknown
- A sense of danger
- A sense of inadequacy

Balancing trust and risk is a process of taking action even when one is not sure of the outcome. Children who exercise a strong will usually take risks in order to accomplish their goals. Even very smart children sometimes get into trouble because they are willing to take risks that violate rules or laws in order to get what they want.

Children with a strong sense of responsibility and respect can achieve their goals without danger to themselves or others. Parents and teachers provide examples for children by their own behaviors and by expecting children to be responsible and respectful.

Hope from Within

A child who is self-confident feels like somebody important. The self-confident child has a sense of hope from within, a belief in possibilities. Such a child views the world with optimism. The child who feels support and encouragement from parents knows that someone cares.

Motivation to Achieve

The self-confident child is motivated and has a desire to take action toward something of value. Motivation, or that inner force to achieve, affects a child's learning and school performance as well as his or her sense of self-worth. Some children seem to be naturally self-motivated. They bubble over with enthusiasm—so much so that sometimes we wish they would slow down! Others need help to get started.

We can make way for children to have successful experiences without interfering or "doing things for them." It's often tempting to show a child how, and it may even be quicker to do it yourself. This can stifle a child's opportunity to work through a problem or complete a task. On the other hand, when a child experiences the excitement of success, motivation provides the energy for the next challenge.

Respect promotes self-confidence. Self-confidence grows when children feel respected by their parents, especially when they have differences in ideas or opinions. A healthy emotional climate is created when parents and children enjoy each other and feel comfortable together. Both parents and children need to express their feelings and thoughts without fear of ridicule. Children who are relaxed with their parents are usually willing to talk about problems and to work at handling conflicts.

Myself

"The pressures of life invade all around. Life escaping the grasp of ordinary individuals. Everybody looks for someone to become. Someone they have seen tackle the challenges of life and come out victorious. Everyone espouses [sic] to be that person, but they forget about themselves. No one wants to be themselves and accept themselves for who they are.

I do not have a mentor because I want not to be like someone else. I want to be myself. I want everyone to accept me for who I am and not what they think I can become.

People must accept themselves for who they are. They must live life how they want to be—not how someone else does."

—Toby R. Jones

Vision and a Sense of Wonder

The successful child enjoys a "sense of wonder" that continues to broaden one's view of the world. Play, poetry, storytelling, story writing, drama, music, and reading open windows to the world for children of all ages. The planet—and indeed, the universe—offers children new dimensions for exploring nature and expanding their ideas. Creative expression and problem solving help children turn difficulties into opportunities and match talent with action.

Children with vision and a sense of wonder generally reflect such characteristics as:

- Inquisitiveness, especially about the "unknown"
- Adventuresomeness—excitement about new challenges
- Enthusiasm about learning, whether at school or elsewhere
- Expressiveness—through the arts, music, dance, poetry, and academics
- Intuitiveness and imagination—thinking in diverse ways, "outside the box"
- The ability to stretch their minds, or consider a wide array of possibilities

There are some things you can change, and there are some things you can never change. We cannot change the weather, the movement of the planets, the color of the sky, the force of ocean waves, how tall your child grows, and how long my nose is. These and many other facets of life we simply accept and learn to live with because they are beyond our control.

On the other hand, we *can* change how we view the world and the unchangeable. Not only can we change, but we can each control much of our own life by:

- How we look at ourselves
- How we look at our children
- How we talk with children
- What we think about life's possibilities
- What we expect of ourselves
- What we expect of our children
- What our state of mind will be
- Sensitivity to ourselves and others

Vision Begins with Imagination

Young children between two and seven years of age envision their world more through their imaginations and fantasies than through logic and reason. Their view of the world is as broad as the stretch of their imaginings.

One of my resident students, a medical doctor studying psychiatry, was intrigued by a kindergartner's knowledge of the "laws of nature." While out on the playground, he asked her how she thought the sun could come up in the East and then go down in the West. He engaged her in conversation:

"How does the sun get from there to there?" he asked, pointing in each direction.

"The sun doesn't really move," she retorted. "It just looks like that."

"You are right," he replied. "But how do you know that?"

"I just know it. The earth moves around and around the sun," she said.

He asked again, "But how do you know that?"

She said, "I know it because I can FEEL it."

"You can feel the earth moving?"

"Yes, I can feel it right now—and I can HEAR it moving."

He said, "You can hear the earth moving? How can you hear it?"

She said, "Yes, I can hear it because I have very good 'earsight.'"

Although the basis of this child's knowledge came from someone's logical explanation of the earth's relationship to the sun, the "proof" came to her by way of her own sensitivity. Her explanation is profoundly personal.

Firsthand Experience

Children learn best when they are directly involved. Play that includes a lot of sensory activity stimulates the brain. For example, experimenting with water and sand encourages children to learn by how things feel as well as by how things look. Learning through the senses puts children in direct contact with the world and how it works. They become a part of the process.

Freedom to simply explore and enjoy nature brings a sense of wonder to a growing mind. Touching, smelling, and gazing at flowers and plants; examining bugs and insects; touching trees; laying in the grass; rolling down hillsides; wading in water; splashing in the waves; wiggling toes in mud; chasing after butterflies; and staring at the stars or clouds are examples of how children broaden their views of the world. Reverence for nature and the planet starts with such play.

Meeting the Challenge

We often assume that evidence of a child's brainpower is reflected in school performance and how a child follows adult logic. Yet sometimes adversity stimulates thinking. A teenager was chastised over and over by her mother for being lazy and for wanting to write silly poems and listen to music. When she was seventeen years old, she was told by her mother that her messy, chaotic room was an indication that she would never amount to anything—that she was destined for failure. The girl became so upset that she said she set her mind to do the best that she could. Within two years, she became an outstanding student and earned a large scholarship to one of the country's top universities. That adverse condition helped her to shape a future filled with possibilities because she believed herself into her own vision.

Expanding One's Vision

A child who grows up with a sense of wonder continues to explore the world and its possibilities. Provide opportunities for your child to be open-minded, sensitive, and aware of life through play, conversation, study, travel, and work. A person who sees lots of options learns to make choices. Talk about possible consequences without telling your child what to do.

Thundering Feet

I could hear the ocean waves rise with heavy thundering feet, and manes blazing in the air

It was a herd of beautiful, wild mustangs, running like thunder

Their bodies were like the lighting in the grayish sky

Their beautiful coats on their skins were glowing with muscles that made my eyes stare

The waves splashed at them; they neighed loudly

I knew that they had feelings inside, running freely while a storm

—Courtney L. Crawford

The Ability to Focus

Success requires the ability to focus on what is important at the moment—whether it's studying for a test, having dinner with a friend, learning to play chess, or engaging in a debate. The person who can focus until the task is complete is on the way to success.

Provide a place for your child to study without intrusions—no TV, radio, phone calls, texting, or people walking in and out. The student who learns to concentrate on a central task will succeed. For example, the successful student aims all energy and thought at solving each problem, answering each question, or writing about each topic, without concern for the possible grade or consequences.

Let children follow their own inclinations. They need time and the freedom to focus on what interests them. They will usually seek challenges and stay with a task as long as they are able to make progress. Allow them to do as much as they can for themselves, giving help only when they invite it or when you see it's needed for encouragement— without instruction or intrusion.

Provide opportunities for children to develop their own talents and unique abilities. For example, a young child who likes music often will play with rhythmic toys and instruments. One who enjoys body movements may lean toward gymnastics, athletics, or objects that nest and stack (eg, cans, bowls, cups, or blocks). Visually stimulated children often like to see balls of various sizes and how they bounce and roll. Some children like to feel textures of paper and cuddly toys. Others like to listen to and read books and play a variety of audio and visual games. Give them time to focus, to immerse themselves in their curiosity. As they get older, talk with them about their interests. Let them know you value their abilities without telling them what to do. Listen to their ideas with a genuine ear.

Make way for children to have enough free space and time to "do their own thing." Avoid interrupting children when you see they are intensely involved, even though they may seem to be just playing. Play provides the best atmosphere for learning during the early years. While they play, children are able to let everything go except what they are engaged in doing at the moment. Children extend their attention spans when they are doing something that captures their interest. Play is the most natural preoccupation for young children and the most appropriate way to explore and learn.

Encourage children to make choices about what to do. When a child is bored, ask questions that help to motivate and get something started. For example, "If you could do anything in the whole world, what would it be?" Or, "If you could work magic, what would you do first?" Then encourage the child to create action that expresses the answers and eliminates the boredom. Sometimes, boredom opens the door to creativity.

Model for children. When you focus until you complete the task, it sets an example for your child. As children observe their own parents, they tend to take on similar values. Parents who leave things undone may be raising their children to do the same. Doing things together provides a natural way of setting examples for staying with tasks until they are finished.

Self-Reflection

Every child needs some private time, to be oneself, and to enjoy a sense of quiet that brings inner peace and reflection. Great ideas, inventions, and problem solving often result when one is quiet and apart from "people traffic" trespassing on the mind.

Daydreaming and Contemplating

Children who daydream reflect on how they are doing. They often go back over their experiences, finding satisfaction or disappointment.

I watched a little boy playing outdoors in a preschool play yard. He soon wandered away from his friends and stood near a big tree. He looked at it and was very quiet. Gradually, he reached out with the spread palm and fingers of one hand, and very gently placed it against the tree. He held it there for several seconds, then drew it back to himself and put it to his chest. I wondered what thoughts and feelings must have been shared with his "tree friend."

Grade school children and teenagers need time for solitude to simply be in a quiet place. They are so often engaged in academic and social activities that rarely do they have time to themselves. Getting "in touch" with themselves is most possible when they are relaxed and alone.

Memories

Young children love to make memory books or scrapbooks. They paste all kinds of pictures and items in their books as reminders of meaningful experiences. They like to draw pictures and make up songs and poems.

Story-making and picture-drawing record children's memories of how they feel and what they think.

Many teenagers keep their own records of what is important to them. These records become treasures that spark memories and reflections. When they review these records, they often make mind connections that take them back in time and space to special events and experiences. Of course, these are very personal and confidential.

Writing and drawing also serve as reflections of feelings and thoughts that may not be pleasant. In fact, some children keep confidential journals or diaries in which they record some of their most intimate feelings about difficult or even dreadful times. Writing poems, songs, and stories also helps children reflect on how they feel. By expressing themselves, they are often able to let go of some of their hurtful feelings. Anger, jealousy, fear, anxiety, frustration, and sadness are only a few of the deep feelings with which children deal. They need ways to face and express these feelings.

Encourage children to use journals and diaries to record what is important to them. Younger children draw pictures and dictate thoughts, while older ones write their own. These records become treasures that spark memories and reflections.

Share time together when children can talk about their ideas, what they have been doing, their wishes, and their feelings. Start a daily ritual of talking together to give children an opportunity to reflect on themselves and how they are doing. As you talk with your child, center on your child's concerns. Listen, and then express your interpretation of what is being said rather than giving your own ideas or advice. Children who develop the ability to look at their accomplishments and their aspirations as well as their difficulties create a foundation of strength rather than a weakness.

Play that includes "tea time," or time for milk and cookies, often sets the pattern for a lifelong ritual of sharing and reflecting.

I Am

I am a girl, and I am deaf.
I wonder who was the first deaf person.
I hear nothing.
I see my sister and brother fighting.

I want more books to read!
I am a girl, and I am deaf.
    I pretend that I am an author.
I feel happy when I read alone.
I touch my birds!
I cry when they do!
I am a girl, and I am deaf.
    I understand lipreading.
I say words with my hands.
I dream that I'm an author.
I try to write good stories.
I hope they will get published someday!
I am a girl, and I am deaf.

—Courtney L. Crawford

CHAPTER 2

Brainpower Unlimited

Whether your child is a toddler or a teenager, you can be sure that brainpower is increasing. Perhaps it makes sense that a baby's head is so much larger than the rest of the body when we know that the brain and nervous system, collectively, grow faster before birth and during the early childhood years than do the muscles and other parts of the body.

By only five years of age, the child's brain is already about nine-tenths the weight it will ever be, and by age ten, it is almost as large as an adult's brain. Even so, it takes about twenty years of maturation before the brain's billions of neurons are fully organized.

Everyday life helps to *integrate*, or bring together, the networking of thoughts and feelings, and action. Children increase their abilities as they encounter new experiences.

One of the most familiar comments made by parents is, "How can these children be learning when all they're doing is playing?" Play actually sets the child up for learning. Smart children like to play. They enjoy learning through their bodies and their minds. For about the first six or seven years of life, children learn best when they are actively using their bodies.

Watch preschoolers as they learn to cut with scissors. Look at their mouths. Tongues are working as hard as hands in manipulating scissor blades. Children cutting out circles often stand up and actually turn around while cutting around circular lines. While children are painting at easels, you see both the tongue and the strokes of the child's brush going up and down. Toddlers trying to open boxes will open their mouths. Minds and bodies work together to solve problems.

Teenagers play, too. They play in more of a "cultural" sense through dance, music, parties, dating, and a host of peer activities.

If we could send the head to school and leave the body at home, we might simplify the process—but that won't happen. We have to learn to live with the whole person, and at times, that poses some pretty tough challenges. The smarter the child, the greater the integration among brain, mind, and body.

The value of integration in a child's development is better understood when we know about the nature and function of the brain. Surely there have been times when you've looked at your child and thought you could see the wheels turning in that brain.

The Human Brain

Despite the fact that the developed modern human brain is at least 50,000 years old, it has only been in the past few decades that we have had the benefit of extensive brain research. Modern neuroscientists are combining their efforts with those in computer science, anthropology, and biomedical science to help unfold the mysteries that lie within the brain.

Basic Brain Functions

The brain serves three basic functions:

- Alertness
- Information processing
- Action

Even newborn babies reflect these three functions. For example, the baby is *alert* to noise, voices, and music. Familiar sounds are *processed* as stimuli, or bits of information, that help babies relax and feel comfortable. When loud or sudden noises occur, a baby may take *action* by screaming or becoming agitated.

As a young school-aged child is playing, these brain functions continue to work together with growing sophistication. Consider Jarrod playing with his friends.

Alertness occurred as Jarrod's eyes looked across the playground and gathered mental clues about what his friends were doing. This *information was processed* as Jarrod registered the sights and sounds of what was going on. *Action* resulted as he leaped forward and ran to join in the fun with his friends.

Brain Organization

Another way to consider the brain's organization is to view it in three layers. Each layer has a special function.

1. **The old brain.** The first layer of the brain believed to have developed in the human is called the old brain. Survival and safety are basic functions of this layer. Body movements and motor control are also centered here. Even tiny babies squirm and wiggle, reach out, and cry to have their needs met—especially when they are hungry or in pain.

2. **The mid-brain.** The second layer of the brain is often called the mid-brain. It houses the limbic system, thought to be the center for emotional responses. When one feels emotions, such as sadness, happiness, excitement, joy, or anger, the limbic system activates neural connections. When one is under extreme pressure, the limbic system may cause the thinking brain to be less efficient. For example, have you ever studied for a test, yet during the test "drawn a blank" on certain questions? Then, when you left the room after the test, the answers suddenly came to you? Your limbic system likely was activated by stress to the degree that it prevented you from thinking at your best. While some pressure and stress may be stimulating, too much may be inhibiting.

Children who develop fears about taking tests or performing in class often are concerned about their parents' or teachers' desires for them to succeed. Such a child may become frustrated and emotionally charged, thereby unable to perform at full capacity—because of the way the brain functions.

3. **The neocortex.** The third, outer layer of the brain appears to be the last to have evolved. This part of the brain is called the neocortex, or new brain. The neocortex comprises about five-sixths of the entire brain. This outer layer is highly developed in humans and accounts for rational, intuitive, and logical thinking.

Right and Left Hemispheres

Within the neocortex, there are two hemispheres, often referred to as the **right brain** and the **left brain.** For the most part, the right brain controls the left, or opposite, side of the body, and the left brain controls the right side of the body. For example, when a stroke occurs in a person's left hemisphere, there is often loss of control of the right arm or leg.

These hemispheres are connected by a dense bridge-like bundle of nerve fibers called the **corpus callosum.** Millions of fibers in the corpus callosum serve as the communication network between the two hemispheres. For example, as a student uses a computer, her corpus callosum carries about four billion impulses per second, thereby making it possible to understand a composition, and also visualize and have feelings about what she is writing.

Children, over several years, gradually gain the full use of the neocortex because the corpus callosum has to go through a process called myelination. It takes about ten years from the time of birth for the nerve tracts to become myelinated, or covered with layers of cellular insulation. Even so, by about age seven, most children have enough myelinated connections between the two hemispheres—through the corpus callosum—to succeed with academic tasks. By this age, most children are able to use logic, read, write, and do arithmetic with a fair amount of ease.

Early on, we see signals in a child's development that let us know there is interaction between the two hemispheres even before maturation is complete. For example, infants learn to crawl using cross-lateral movements. That is, the right arm and the left leg work as a unit, while the left arm and the right leg work in unison. This is one of the early signs that brain development is on target. Additional evidence comes with the preschooler learning to ride a tricycle, with legs working alternately, yet in a unified way.

Left-Hemisphere Functions

Even though the two hemispheres are connected by the corpus callosum, they each have different functions. In general, the left hemisphere seems to be organized for processing one stimulus (or bit of information or experience) at a time. This leads to an **orderly sequence and pattern** in thinking and doing. **Auditory stimuli** (hearing) appear to be processed through the left brain, an indication of why children learn to say what they hear. Examples of left-brain functions are:

- Language and speech
- Numbers and values
- Reasoning with logic
- Analyzing and organizing

Right-Hemisphere Functions

In contrast to the left side of the brain, the right hemisphere processes *clusters of stimuli* simultaneously. That is, lots of information or experience can be dealt with at the same time. This makes it possible to handle ideas even before they are understood, to grasp a sense of what is happening, and to "roll with the punches." **Visual stimuli** are processed through the right hemisphere. Perhaps that is why many children copy, or do what they see others doing. This right-brain clustering enables such functions as:

- Intuition
- Imagination
- Body movements
- Music and creative expression
- Art and design
- Flexibility
- Spontaneity

Children Think Differently Than Adults

Children, for about the first seven to ten years, tend to be dominated more by the right hemisphere than the left. This right-brain dominance accounts for children being so spontaneous, active, and visually stimulated.

Let's take an example of how kindergartners use their right hemispheres. Mandi can escort you from home to the nearby school, going around corners and up streets. But she cannot draw a map showing you how to get there. The right brain makes possible a "mind map," or picture, for her. Later, as she matures, the left hemisphere will work together with the right to enable her to draw a map, precisely showing each turn, including the north, east, south, and west directions.

Long before the left brain is ready to organize symbols into words and sentences, the right hemisphere enables children to give meaning to clusters of information that come in the form of pictures and images. A preschool child may look at pictures in a book and make up stories before reading skills are achieved. This young child also can do little dances and move in rhythmic patterns to music. Drawing and art activities are means of expressing ideas and feelings.

As children have new experiences, the right brain enables them to shape the unfamiliar into meaningful image patterns, or mind pictures. For example, children can play musical instruments by ear, without formal training. They can draw pictures before they can read or write.

Do Boys and Girls Think Differently?

Adults aside, let's consider how boys and girls think during the first seven to ten years of life. There is a difference. Boys, during these early years, tend to be more partial to right-brain functions in their actions, whereas girls are more inclined to follow left-brain tendencies.

Boys tend to "think through their bodies" with impulsive and spontaneous actions. They are visually stimulated—they see something and go after it. They waste no time in wanting to get their hands on something to examine and try out. Boys are very sensitive and intuitive during these early years. Many mothers report that boys can sense when they don't feel well or when something is wrong. Because boys learn while they are "on the move," they often get into trouble in kindergarten and first grade. Many boys have difficulty sitting still for long periods of time. They also tend to pay more attention to a teacher's body language than to what is being said. When first learning to write, most boys form their letters in a hodgepodge fashion, unconcerned about precise order and shape. Is it any wonder that so many more boys than girls are referred for learning disabilities in the early years of school? And all along, they are simply following the natural tendencies of right-brain activity.

Girls tend to favor left-brain functions during the early years. Most kindergarten and first-grade girls can sit still, listen, and follow instructions with little difficulty. They form their letters precisely and carefully in an orderly manner. Girls are inclined to be more logical and less flexible early on. For example, one mother reported that her five-year-old daughter, Karen, and four-year-old son, Cliff, looked forward to going to the zoo one Saturday. Then, that Saturday, she did not feel well. On top of that, it was raining. Cliff came in and said, "Mom, are you mad at me? Are you upset?" She explained she wasn't feeling well, and since it was raining, maybe the zoo trip would have to be on another day. Cliff responded by saying, "Mom, I don't want you to be sick." Then entered Karen, who stood firmly and said, "Mom, we have to go to the zoo." Mom gave the same explanation, to which Karen replied, "But Mom, you promised. Now it's Saturday, and we have to go to the zoo!"

Whole-Brain Thinking

Eventually, maturation leads to left and right hemispheres interacting to bring about whole-brain thinking. When this occurs, children are able to create stories, draw pictures about them, and write words to express ideas and orders of events.

As the left and right hemispheres work together, reading and writing become natural abilities. Some examples that children have whole-brain capacity are when they can tie their shoes, can balance on a bicycle enough to ride without help, and know that changing the shape of a piece of play dough does not change the amount of it.

A child who takes violin lessons before the hemispheres are working together may be able to follow the notes by what they look like rather than by what they mean. Some children, on the other hand, are able to play by "ear." Only when the whole brain interacts does the child know how to read music and what to do while sensing the overall effect of the tone, rhythm, and quality of sound produced.

By about age ten, most connections between right and left hemispheres are working well. Generally, by the end of adolescence, or even by about age sixteen, myelination is fairly complete, and children are ready for advanced forms of thinking.

Brain Spurts

While development refers to the gradual unfolding of maturation and potential, it is not always smooth and even. There are now scientific indications that spurts occur in brain development. That is, development seems to burst forth with greater intensity at some periods and level, or even decline, at other periods. As we observe children, we see evidence of what appears to be spurts in brain development from infancy through adolescence.

First Spurt

Between ages *three and ten months*, there appears to be evidence of a spurt of brain development that propels the infant forward in mental and motor abilities. Babies learn to roll over, sit up, pull up, grasp and play with objects, recognize parents, and use vocalizations and crying to get attention. Memory is intact by about nine months, and the world takes on a whole new meaning.

Second Spurt

During the *third year*, children show a marked excitement about learning. Speech is developing rapidly, toilet training is mastered, body coordination improves by leaps and bounds, independence is well under way, and imagination is unleashed.

Third Spurt

At about *age five*, the right hemisphere seems to be developing rapidly, while the left hemisphere seems to plateau, or remain somewhat static. This may account for why children are capable of intuitive, rather than logical, thinking. Their bodies play an active role as they learn by doing, express feelings openly, and interact with others joyfully, moving about from one place to another. Kindergarten finds children enjoying artwork because they can express their impressions. They are naturally curious and learn in spontaneous ways. Their bodies and their senses still lead their minds.

During this same time, left-hemisphere development appears to be in a relatively calm state. This may be the reason why so many children are unable to read with ease; have difficulty with abstractions, such as number values; and lack the logic required for many academic tasks.

Fourth Spurt

By *age seven,* a new brain spurt propels the child toward logical thinking with the ability to read, write, and do arithmetic with relative ease. This is a period of excitement about collecting information and wanting to know about everything. Memorizing is not only easy, but it's also fun.

Fifth Spurt

Age eleven brings evidence of another spurt that pushes the child into abstract thinking. When this occurs, the child moves beyond concrete ways of solving problems to being able to hypothesize and simultaneously consider numerous possibilities.

Sudden Decline

At *about age thirteen,* the brain seems to take a dive "below the line," with little activity that supports academics. Children at this stage tend to be preoccupied with the many changes going on in their bodies.

They look at themselves and wonder, *What's happening to me?* Boys have hair growing on their faces, voices are changing, and the body is growing by leaps and bounds. Girls find themselves in new body shapes, and emotions seem to be more fragile than ever. There is great interest in the opposite sex. And who has any energy left for studies? For some, this decline, or "nose dive," in brain development occurs as early as twelve; for others, it may be as late as age fourteen. This is the time for parents to back off, be patient, and look forward to the next spurt.

Sixth Spurt

By about *age fifteen,* another spurt of brain development seems to occur, which moves the child to a new level of thinking. There is more sophistication for considering others' viewpoints. A sense of responsibility is coupled with the ability to take charge of one's own thinking. School becomes a place for serious effort in academics. Advanced academics are more acceptable as challenges to be met rather than requirements to be avoided.

As we consider these brain spurts, we must keep in mind that a great variation exists among individuals. Some children are ready for writing and reading by kindergarten age because at four, they experienced the plateau of the left hemisphere, and by five, it moved into an upward path. The point of this discussion is to recognize that many changes occur in the human body as maturity and development unfold. While we cannot know exactly what goes on inside the body—nor can we change it—we can be considerate of the outside manifestations.

Flexibility in school programs is the key to success for children, especially in the kindergarten, and first- and second-grade levels. There are great variations in rates of development among children during these early years of school, and therefore curricula need to be designed to meet a wide range of abilities and skills.

Integrated Learning

Children have the brain capacity by about age seven to succeed in school. By age ten, most children are capable of making A's and B's. Success is usually imminent when children practice integrated learning. When the old brain is satisfied by ritual and repetition, children feel safe and secure about their new and challenging experiences. When the midbrain, with its limbic system, regulates emotional stress, children are stimulated, yet not immobilized, to balance risk with confidence. As the corpus callosum plays its vital role in combining right- and left-hemisphere functions, children are capable of learning to think with a full range of possibilities, from intuition to objective logic. Integration, or bringing together the interactions of the whole brain, offers children excitement and satisfaction as they master the art of thinking and performance.

One might ask, "If human brains go through the same kind of development and maturation process, why don't all children progress in their academic skills at the same rate?" Good question.

Every child is a little different. Even identical twins soon show their unique characteristics by the way they each behave and respond to those around them. Just as people are different on the outside, they also are unique on the inside. We may share common elements of being human, but the rate at which we progress and how we use our humanness vary with each of us.

My Teacher

—Homework, homework, homework—what a terrible day!

Thousands of homework assignments would take me thousands of years to do

That was the reason I hated my teacher; she gives thousands of homework assignments.

Math, science, social studies, English, writing—what terrible work to do! My hands die from writing too much, and my arms become tired, my eyes begin to get sleepy, my legs and feet start to feel strange, and I snore; I never wake up in thousands of years because I have thousands of homework assignments that take thousands of years to do!

"Math, science, social studies, English, writing!" she says as she passes out those terrible papers again. I AM GOING TO DIE!

—Courtney L. Crawford

CHAPTER 3

Growing
Up Smart

S mart from the beginning—infants to adolescents—children make you laugh, cry, scream, and at times want to pull your hair out! They also make you want to jump for joy, and they, like no other creatures, can bring sunshine into your heart on the darkest of days.

Children have the rare ability to know when you are most vulnerable. As if they have invisible antennae, they are able, at any given moment, to sense your mood, your level of stress, your level of tolerance—and your breaking point.

They also sense when you need a respite—when you are suffering from a headache or have had a bad day. They "back off" when you can't take any more. They seem to know that you're not up to their usual challenges. So they give you some time and space, but they also send an unspoken message: "I expect you to be back to feeling good soon."

These masterminds can handle just about anything that comes their way—for good or for bad. They have such powerful imaginations; they simply turn on their inside "video studios" and create scenarios that make it possible to handle in fantasy whatever they cannot manage in reality. And unfortunately for some, they carry out their fantasies with tragic endings. Two young boys, filled with fear and desperation, shot and killed their abusive father while he slept. But on the positive side, there are thousands of untold stories about children who save lives and prevent disasters. Recently, a five-year-old girl saw her father choking and knew he had to have help. She had the knowledge to dial 911. The emergency operator instructed her to unlock the front door to the house and then stay on the line until the emergency team arrived. This child's presence of mind in time of crisis unquestionably saved her father's life.

Young children are smart enough to work video games, computers, iPads, and other electronic devices. They are smart enough to work complicated puzzles and play "brain games." They are also smart enough to load and use guns. So regardless of how smart children are, they still need the loving support and consistent firm guidance that comes from caring parents and teachers.

Infants Are Incredible

Smart from the Start

While babies are bundles of joy, they are also demanding of your time and attention. The day a newborn enters your life, everything changes. Not only do you shift gears with your social and work life, but your personal family life takes a dramatic turn as well. Suddenly, your whole routine and pattern of behavior is being influenced by the most dependent member of the family! Others may have to wait, feel ignored, be bypassed, and mount their own defenses against your devotion to the newest love of your life. This baby now places you in the most strategic role of your entire life—that of being a parent!

Your baby's intelligence is off to a great start with her brain already one-fourth the size that it will be when fully mature. Compare that to a body that is only about 5 percent of its mature size. Such potential! And you will be in charge of directing much of that potential during the next few years. Such responsibility!

Human infants depend on parents longer than other species of living creatures do. While some animals begin to walk and seek their own food within a few days of birth, your baby will need your help for months and months. Perhaps this strengthens attachment as parent and baby experience a closeness never to be repeated in the same way.

Even so, babies are not completely helpless. In fact, your newborn manages to get your attention by a single piercing sound that goes right to the heart of your consciousness. And this call can get you up and moving even from the depths of deep sleep. Just as powerful as the onset of a cry for help, your baby can look at you with those big, bright, sparkling eyes and capture your heart and soul.

So How Do Babies Think?

For the first six months, babies think mostly in feelings and sensations. Their tummies hurt when they are hungry, so they cry. They sense the warmth and comfort of a parent holding them, and they relax.

As early as a few weeks old, babies become sensitive to their parents. They seem to know when they are present and when they aren't. They use their senses particularly for hearing and smelling and touching. A baby can feel the texture of the parent's skin while being cuddled and held.

Since babies can hear by the age of five months of prenatal development, they are quite familiar with parents' voices. Many fathers report talking to their babies in utero, and soon after they are born, babies are responsive to their fathers' voices. Of course, a mother's voice often brings comfort to the most distressed newborn.

An example of how sensitive babies are is their crying during air travel. They sense the difference in pressure on their bodies and the vibrations brought on by the plane's movement through the air. During takeoff and landing, babies often scream as a way of balancing the pressure in their ears. Since these changes in the environment are unfamiliar, the baby lets others know about it. Parents are often embarrassed, and their anxiety flows over to the baby and can make the situation worse instead of better. Babies sense the tension in their parents and respond by exaggerated body movements and crying—or screaming. Of course, they are also able to settle down and adapt to changes fairly readily because they actively process stimulation through the right hemispheres in their brains.

Babies gradually think in mind pictures, or images. For example, by the age of about nine months, they can hold an image of the parent in mind.

They know the difference between parents and friends. They often cry when the parent leaves as a way of saying, "I'd rather have you than anyone else." Again, they are able to settle and adapt to caregivers and relatives who are kind and gentle. Holding a mental image of the absent parent also may give them a sense of comfort—at least for a while.

Is the Universe Friendly?

Babies who get started in life with more good feelings than bad ones tend to develop patterns that reflect positive attitudes about you and the world in which they live. When their mental picture books are filled with beautiful images, they tend to look at you and the world as beautiful. On the other hand, babies who carry a lot of ill feelings begin to fear the world, and when their mind pictures are unpleasant ones, they may develop behaviors to fight against these.

Watch tiny babies and their parents when they play together. It's like a dance or tai chi. The baby and parent synchronize with each other. When the parent talks to the baby, the baby mimics the mouth movements. When the baby smiles, the parent smiles; when the parent's head moves, so does the baby's—the dance continues. When babies get tired or have had enough stimulation with such play, they give a signal, like turning the head or body away, as if to say, "I've had enough."

Babies communicate not only with body movements, but with facial expressions, too. For example, when babies take nourishment, they let parents know when they have had enough. They give clear messages by closing the mouth or spitting out the food. They also may present an awful scowl and turn the head away.

Isn't it wonderful that parents can intuitively read their babies' messages that come from babbling, facial gestures, and body language? But isn't it even more remarkable that babies can read their parents' faces and body language? And they seem to know what their parents are saying by the tones and qualities of their voices—long before the stages of speech set in.

Babies Influence Parenting Styles

Babies play a major role in helping parents develop parenting styles. For example, a parent is easily stimulated when approaching a baby who shows a big smile, gurgles and coos, and blinks bright eyes that sparkle with delight. Such interactions bring about a close bonding between the baby and parent. Such responses also entice the parent to play with the baby a lot because it's such a joy. In contrast, think of what may happen to a parent who approaches a baby who has a mental disability. If the baby does not respond to the parent's approach, the parent is likely to back away. If it becomes too uncomfortable, the parent may feel inadequate. Such babies may be unwittingly deprived of the stimulation they need because there is not that natural cycle of interaction triggered by natural response patterns.

Adapting to Caregivers

The question continues to loom: What about placing babies in the care of someone other than their parents? Parents who secure high-quality care can relax and temporarily "let go" of children. Babies, as well as young children, are quite adaptable. This is another remarkable feature about them: They respond to people who are trustworthy and caring. Your baby can "tell" you more about caregivers than anyone else. They have the capacity to sense when someone is comfortable with them. They know, by intuitive wisdom, that a person either cares or doesn't. They also sense the genuine response and guidance provided by caregivers. These babies and young children are not concerned about credentials or degrees, but they are astutely aware of the nature of the relationships between themselves and others. They are content to be cared for by those who are genuinely interested in their overall well-being.

Parents Are the First Teachers

You are, without exception, the most powerful teacher your child will ever have. The influence you have may be subtle and spoken with body and facial gestures as much as with your words, but it is dynamic. The "proof of the pudding" is in the child's memory. Children rarely remember their early caregivers, but they always remember the feelings and nuances of growing up with their parents. Caregivers can supplement the family, but they can never take the place of a parent—not a single parent, a working parent, or any other parent. Children are simply too smart for that to happen.

When you feel comfortable in your role as a parent, your child will make progress as rapidly as nature will allow. Since you have no control over your child's rate of maturity, there's no need to rush things along.

Relax, and enjoy the growing years, and take comfort in the notion that **your child is smarter than you think**.

Toddlers Are Terrific Thinkers!

Toddlers can be like cuddly kittens one minute and tenacious tigers the next. Depending on what they're after, they have the ability to shift gears and make a 180-degree turnaround, bypassing all caution signals or stop signs. Their minds are like steel traps, and they sense when it's time to move in and take over.

Contrary to the more conventional view of toddlers as the "terrible twos," a more accurate term is "terrific thinkers." The very fact that they give parents such a rough time indicates they are thinking—even though at times they may be conniving and cantankerous.

Between about eighteen and twenty-four months, toddlers go through a dramatic change from being infants to becoming children. The greatest leap in development is their marked increase in intellectual capacity. Two major milestones are, first, the ability to mentally manipulate, or think about, a possible outcome of "if I do this, then this will happen"; and second, the capacity to invent new ways of doing things. As an example, the toddler pulls a toy by a string, then dangles it, and then slings it around and around. The very fact they are inventive indicates that imagination and creative thinking are active. The more difficult their behavior, the smarter they are—that's the consolation for parents.

Having mastered the skills for walking, running, and climbing, they now head for discovery and invention by exploring everything in sight—or anything within range of their vast imaginations. Favorite pastimes include dumping things out of boxes, pulling things off of shelves, and throwing things on the floor—including food! They would rather crawl in a box than keep their toys in it. Or climb to the cupboard where they think the cookies are hiding.

Cause and Effect

The law of cause and effect begins to take shape in the mind of the toddler. Such behaviors as scratching and biting suddenly emerge without warning. The toddler realizes that a scratch or bite causes a dramatic change in someone else's behavior. Visions of power and control suddenly bring the mind and body into synchronized action, and the toddler has just learned how to manipulate others! Watch out, nothing is safe from this point forward.

Forbidden and fascinating items are the most tempting targets. Toddlers can invent elaborate "ladders" to reach what they are after, whether it's the fish food, sister's new doll, or mom's computer mouse.

They have incredible ability to focus until they get what they want. And if nothing else works, they may scream or throw themselves on the floor with a display of body movements and vocal intonations unique to the universe—all because they are smart. A myriad of seemingly random events—pushing TV or computer buttons, taking pages out of books, pulling yarn from a rug—actually give toddlers a strong sense of power and of being in control.

Reason Is Anchored in Imagination and Fantasy

Many parents report that their toddlers suddenly refuse to take a bath. One father said his twenty-month-old always enjoyed bath time. She was delighted to splash and play and had to be dragged from the tub. Then one evening, without any warning, she screamed and refused to get into the tub. He said he tried every way he knew and finally gave up. I suggested that he give her a doll and let her bathe it. Then, let her pull the plug and watch the water swirl out, leaving the doll safely in the tub. Perhaps her fear of bathing was brought on by imagining that she would swirl down the drain with the water. As she played, she identified with the doll, and she could see that the water disappeared without the doll, and she could see that the doll was safe. Her father reported that the problem was solved. But most of all, he was excited that she was growing intellectually and was not just being stubborn.

Another signal that imagination is intact is when a toddler awakens from a nap or from sleeping and screams for no apparent reason. More than likely, the child has been dreaming and awakens from a "different world." After a few minutes, all is calm, especially when familiar people are there to anchor the child in the real world. During the night, a parent's gentle voice is often enough to help the child settle and return to sleep.

Toddlers and Telephones

On the one hand, toddlers enjoy playing with telephones, either real ones or toys. While pretending, they carry on elaborate conversations. They love pretending with a parent or caregiver, and can carry on and on and on. On the other hand, they often become upset when a parent is talking on the phone to someone they cannot see. Why such a change? First, toddlers are often confused when they see an adult talking to an inanimate object. The toddler's thinking is something like this: *While it is okay for me to play, mom knows better. Why is she doing that?* Second, toddlers don't like to see a parent devote so much attention to a phone conversation that does not include them. They feel shut out. So they begin to invent ways to get the parent off the phone. If all else fails, some hold their breath, and that usually works.

Toddlers and Temptations

We can never be too careful when it comes to protecting toddlers. Since they are so smart, it's almost impossible to guard against the maneuverings thought of by their ingenious minds. However, there are precautions that can prevent serious disasters. For example, we can avoid hiding cookies and other forbidden items in dangerous places. One child climbed on top of the stove to get to the cabinet above and burned to death.

All electrical outlets can be covered with safety plugs, and extension cords can be kept out of any possible reach of toddlers. Cleaning fluids and other toxic substances must be stored in places that are locked and out of the child's range of exploration.

The kitchen is not only a fascinating learning center for toddlers; it's also the most dangerous place. Examples of temptations for toddlers are pots of hot food on the stove with handles they can grab and pull down, or knives and sharp objects they can experiment with while playing.

One mother, now in therapy, told a tragic story that has left its mark on her family for life. Having almost completed a beautiful bedspread she had been crocheting for months, she left her needlework on the living room sofa while she responded to the signal of the oven timer and did a few tasks in the kitchen. Upon returning to the living room, she was awestruck to see that her toddler had pulled the yarn from the bedspread, creating a mound of crimped nothingness. In a rage of fury, she grabbed the child and threw him against the wall. Permanent brain damage was the irreversible result of leaving temptation unattended.

Oppositional Undertakings

The major mark of distinction that identifies a typical toddler is oppositional behavior: You suggest, and the child resists; you guide, and the child turns away; you insist, and the child retreats; you demand, and the child wages war. Needless to say, this is the "empathy time" for parents! Even though this oppositional phase may be the most challenging period for parents, it is by far the greatest lodestone in the young child's intellectual acumen.

Evolution into a person, separate and apart from the parent, is thrust upon the toddler's mind, body, and spirit. "It's time for me to demonstrate that I can make it on my own—so get out of the way, world, because here I come!" This is when they strike out on their own, trying to do everything their way. As children become more aware of themselves as separate people, they begin to test limits. They quickly learn how many times Mom will say, "Stop!" before she loses patience.

Forget the toilet training during this oppositional phase. Wait a few months, and this, too, shall pass. As the child moves beyond oppositional behavior, you will be amazed and relieved to see the cooperation that looms ahead.

Toddlers Are Talkers

One- and two-word sentences are backed up by lots of intellectual grunts and articulate body language. By this time, the toddler shifts from echolalia to monologue; that is, from repeating the last word heard to talking to be heard. The speech category of monologue is mastered as the toddler begins to talk for the sheer pleasure of hearing his or her own voice. Observe, and you will find them talking to toys, furniture, and themselves. There doesn't have to be anyone present—at least not anyone we would recognize! Within a few months, the toddler's language and speech increase enormously and communicating becomes one more way to gain control. Lots of new words are invented, too, especially while toddlers are "reading" to themselves.

Since this is such prime time for language and speech, parents and caregivers can help by spending time reading to toddlers. Sitting close brings a sense of comfort and emotional bonding. Later, children will reach for books—as much for the psychological attachment to the ones they love as for the books themselves.

As for **pacifiers**, this is the time to throw them away. Toddlers who are motivated to talk need to be free to let the words roll off the tongue. Pacifiers inhibit speech. So what about thumb-sucking and its impact on speech? They are not the same. A child will simultaneously remove a thumb while saying a word, but that's not so with a pacifier, which requires deliberate action. The brain works rapidly and won't wait for the delay.

And speaking of speech, words bring about action for young children. The brain responds immediately to action words. Say the word "throw," and it is done! Since the brain is still maturing, what we say to a young child is processed differently than what we say to an adult. For example, negative contractions are not processed as rapidly as action verbs. When you say to a child, "Don't step in that mud," the brain hears that, but processes, "STEP in that mud." Don't throw that sand" becomes "THROW that sand." So, "Do as I say" works best when we take the positive approach of WHAT TO DO rather than what *not* to do. "Walk around the puddle" and "Pour the sand gently" are good examples.

Preschool Potentials

Brace yourself for a burst of potential genius. Children between about three and six years of age may think with their heads, but their necks provide the pivotal position that connects bodies, brains, and feelings. Never again will there be such an intriguing period of rapid development with logic created from intuition and mental images carried by the imagination beyond the outer limits of reality. The preschooler's potential can be enhanced by loving concern and sensitive support of parents and teachers, or it can be shattered by overindulgence on the one hand or neglect on the other. For example:

Adam: "Mom, why can't I stay up late?"
Mom: "Well, okay, on Friday night, you may stay up late."
(Friday at about 10 p.m.)
Mom: "It's getting late, and I think you have been up long enough. You need to get ready for bed now."
Adam: "Mom, is it late?"

Mom: "Yes, quite late!"

Adam: "Does that mean *really* late?"

Mom: "Yes. And you need to get ready for bed."

Adam: "But Mom, you said I could stay up late . . . and if it's late, then I can stay up."

This is a period of learning through play, of free expression and experimentation. Children are so genuine at this stage, yet so fanciful.

Vision and a Sense of Wonder

Preschoolers build their potential for success by expanding their vision and sense of wonder. You can see it in their eyes. You can hear it in their voices. You can sense it in their body movements. Empowerment grows for them through imaginative thinking.

Several years ago, while waiting to see a man about a business matter, I met his beautiful five-year-old granddaughter. We began to visit, and soon she was reciting to me, hardly taking a breath, a half-hour version of Rumpelstiltskin. I can still see her in my mind's eye as she so exquisitely dramatized every line with vocal intonations and body gestures I never knew were possible for such a young child. She became such a part of the story that she seemed almost transcended. What potential looms ahead for her!

Fantasy is at the heart of their sense of wonder. They believe what they see—whether in their mind's eye or in reality. They are capable of making up pretend friends and animals that become a part of their play. And sometimes they want to bring them to the dinner table! So how do we handle these fantasy friends?

First of all, having imaginary playmates is perfectly natural at this stage. While it's normal for a child to carry on a conversation with or give instructions to this invisible creature, it's not normal for us to do so—unless we qualify our participation. That is, we can say, "Do you want me to pretend with you for a while?" If the answer is yes, then we can pretend for a few minutes, after which time we say something like, "It's time for me to stop pretending now. You may continue to play." That's all it takes. Children seem to sense that adults are beyond having imaginary playmates, yet they are comfortable with such activity.

Most preschoolers simply need freedom to play, and they will find something to do. Out of boredom, they can create excitement. Play that is filled with firsthand experiences keeps the sense of wonder expanding. Examples are water and sand play, dramatic and dress-up play, outdoor play, and the use of a wide variety of materials, such as play dough, clay, paper and paste, cloth scraps, and painting materials. Drawing, storytelling, and story-making open new windows to the child's world.

Books and Stories

Language and speech skills increase by leaps and bounds when parents and caregivers share reading and story time with young children. The more involved the child, the broader the stretch of the mind. Be receptive to their questions and comments, and let them embellish the stories. They are old enough now to care for their own books with a proper place to keep them when they are not being used. Such habits help children develop lifelong respect for property as well as regard for books and reading.

Sit close to children while reading together in order to strengthen the bond between you, personally, and between the child and the idea of reading. They will come back over and over for more reading—and most of the time they will snuggle in for close encounters of the best kind.

The Time for Tall Tales

Preschoolers are primed for telling tall tales, or for twisting the truth. These are far from deliberate lies, but they are close to how life is viewed from within the mind of the child. We can usually feel more comfortable about children's stories when we respond with a qualifying statement such as, "My, you have a wonderful imagination. I like the way you make up stories."

There are times, of course, when children make up the stories to protect themselves. If necessary, they'll blame the spilled milk on George, the imaginary cat. There are other times when they are sincere as can be in their fantasies.

I cherish the recollection of a young mother who told me about a Saturday morning incident with her four- and five-year-old boys. While cleaning the house, she found two moldy sausages in a "butlers' helper" on the corner table in the living room. She was furious and determined to discover which child committed this foul play. So she carried the container, which looked much like a frying pan with a lid on it, out to the back patio. She called her boys from their play and was about to ask who did it when the younger child blurted out ever so spontaneously, "I think they're done, don't you?"

Music and the Arts

Lasting impressions and brain patterns often are set during the preschool period. Children who listen to classical music, for example, likely will appreciate it the rest of their lives. Becoming familiar with great paintings and sculptures and the artists who created them is natural for young children. They need only be exposed. While it is true that many children resist going to art museums when there are other activities they'd rather do, once inside, they are often fascinated. One grandmother told me that when her grandchildren came to visit her in New York, she always "dragged" them to the museums. As they grew into adulthood and continued to visit, they always wanted to go to the museums.

Art and music form the foundation for learning because children are open to visual and spatial stimulation as well as sound effects. You can see the rhythm in their bodies when they move to music, and they love to dance and sing. Repetition through music sets up patterns for practicing a variety of skills later, including math and reading.

Drawing and painting are the forerunners to writing. Displaying a child's pictures lets them know they are valued. When children respect their own creations, they are encouraged to expand their ideas and feelings through these art forms.

As for painting, lots of parents view this as the messiest and most difficult activity to manage. One mother, determined to find a way to lessen the task of managing this form of art, decided to turn the bathtub into an art studio. She knew this would solve the problem because any spills could simply be washed down the drain and paintings could be left to dry before displaying them. She placed a box in the bathtub for use as an easel between her two daughters, ages three and five years. Then, she had them strip down to their undies, climb in, and paint. After about twenty minutes, she went in to check on them, fully expecting them to have painted several works of art on the large newsprint sheets she had provided. Not so! What she found, instead, was two girls "tattooed" from the neck down. After gasping from shock, she was about to scream with frustration when the older child looked up at her and said, "Oh, Mommy, this is the most fun I ever had in my whole life!"

Tricks and Trivia

Magicians have little over preschoolers' ability to "pull rabbits out of the hat" when they want their own way. From tantrums to make-believe, they try every trick they know when the issue is in their best interest. There are probably enough preschool tricks for the *Guinness World Records* book when it comes to finding a way to sleep in the parent's bed. Preschoolers think of everything, from monsters in the closet to bugs in the bed. And why not? From their perspective, what better place to be safely tucked away than in the warm and cozy comfort of the biggest bed in the house—with snuggles next to the biggest and best in the family? So what can parents do to prevent these tricks from becoming routine patterns?

Approach the issues, like the sleeping problem, from the child's point of view: "I know you wish you could sleep in my bed. What would it be like?" Listen to the child, and then set the limit. "Do you want me to tuck you into your bed, or do you want to do it yourself?" Then, follow through. If the child says there are monsters to fear, play into the child's fantasy: "If you imagine there are monsters, you can imagine that your teddy bear can stand guard for you." Or, "Maybe you can pretend to get rid of those monsters by putting them to sleep under the trees." Children at this stage often count on parents to set and enforce limits because they can't. Even when children push and test the limits, they feel safe when parents enforce them. When children know they can count on their parents to stop them, they learn how far they can go.

Social Butterflies

Children at this stage enjoy having others around them, children and adults alike. All one has to do is enter the scene, and they will take over.

Soon they engage you in their dramatic and imaginative play, reflecting their intellectual abilities and practicing their social skills. They delight in talking and often get carried away with letting you know just how adept they are.

Yet they are caught in somewhat of a dilemma: On the one hand, they want to be part of the group, and on the other hand, they want to be independent. As they progress toward the school-age years, they gradually grow out of their self-protective cocoons and begin to emerge into autonomous, yet social, beings—ready for new horizons that will challenge their rapidly maturing minds.

School-Age Scholars

Entry into kindergarten or first grade provides a new and challenging backdrop that impacts each child's self-image. Children begin to see themselves as *scholars*, ready to take on tasks that will tax their minds and spark their spirits for new ways of learning and approaching life.

Latency, the developmental period between about age seven and twelve years, marks an era of transition in which the child shifts emphasis from family involvement to the school and community. Two major social groups comprise latency: *school* and *peers*. Latency often is called the "school-age" period because children are judged on their performance and academic merits. Up to now, they have been accepted as family members regardless of their performance. Now, the child is a representative of the family in these social settings.

Major Tasks of Latency
The major tasks of latency include:

- **To achieve acceptance and status in school.** Teachers evaluate children on the basis of their individual achievements and performance, according to impersonal scales. Realization of this new way of life can be threatening to many children.
- **To measure up to one's level of self-confidence.** One's personality undergoes considerable reorganization. That is, the child develops new abilities to prepare for living within the larger society outside the home and child-care community.

Latency is also a time of *transition* between the closing of the prelogical, intuitive, and imaginative thinking to the logical, rational, and objective world. Now, children must master the art of thinking for themselves.

Even so, they are still primarily concrete thinkers. Their conversations reflect how literally they interpret what they hear. For example, a third-grader hearing his parents talk about their high school senior wanting to pursue marine biology interrupted with, "I didn't know that Marines studied biology."

Children in latency are in a state of relative calm. They shift their energy and interests to activities outside the family, especially to peer relations and to learning. This is probably the easiest time for parents in relationships. But beware—it's often the calm before the storm of adolescence!

Attachments are now divided among parents, teachers, and peers. There is much less turmoil at home because the child is preoccupied with school and friends. While children pursue new relationships, they still enjoy closeness with their parents.

The child takes active interest in schoolwork, projects, hobbies, community activities, and friendships. A child who has difficulty making this shift may develop feelings of inferiority and a fear of failure. Behavior problems or problems related to learning may result unless children have support from teachers and parents.

Proving One's Own Merit

Some children at this stage exhibit a compulsive striving to excel. They seek competition to "prove" their merit. Too much self-imposed pressure can bring loss of perspective. A child may develop unrealistic expectations and become more ambitious than he or she is capable of handling.

One's self-concept, when adequate, serves to regulate these ambitions and prevents temptations for unrealistic competition. A strong sense of self enables the child to consider the reaction of others as well as one's own desires.

Personal and Social Integration

Latency is a time for learning "WHO I AM" while at the same time learning about society's value system. New sets of ideas begin to alter the child's viewpoint. One is now able to move beyond the self-centered and family-centered expectations of early childhood to a broader view of the world.

The child experiences a major pull in loyalties. There is a shift from family loyalty to school and peers. This may cause feelings of ambivalence toward parents and siblings. The child has such thoughts as *Why do I feel this way? Am I wrong?* They still need lots of support from their parents to make these social transitions.

This is a time for developing a sense of responsibility and qualities of leadership. The child begins to assume a place in society.

Fantasy Still Abounds

Some children tend to repress unacceptable impulses or fantasy wishes. They suddenly take opposite reactions, such as having great concerns about a parent's health, especially after having had fantasies of revenge or anger. They engage in rituals that magically "undo" a wish or say prayers to "make things right." Fantasy still helps the latency child compensate for feelings of inadequacy. Imagined accomplishments help motivate a child to work hard in school or with some community effort. Some children may lie about grades or performance, hoping parents will not discover the truth. They don't want to disappoint teachers or adults and will do almost anything to avoid humiliation.

Fun and Games

Never again will children have the advantage of being smart enough to express themselves with logical thought, yet innocent enough to be excused for their exceptional misbehaviors. They enjoy a myriad of games, social activities, and peer interactions. From "brain games" to slumber parties, their minds and mouths rarely stop. Silliness can be the order of the day as they try to outdo one another with their rhymes and riddles. A typical example: "If runners get athlete's foot, what do astronauts get? Missile-toe!"

School-Related Problems

Latency is filled with challenges for both parents and their children. Smart children often suffer because they have insight and are especially sensitive to new expectations. They often exercise their creativity in order to avoid facing uncomfortable situations. Rather than be humiliated at school for not having their homework finished, they find clever ways to distract the teacher or get sympathy. Some of them would rather be reprimanded for misbehavior than for poor academic performance. Some children are afraid to ask for help because they think it means they will be viewed as failures.

Talking with children about their fears and feelings may be sufficient to prevent such serious problems as school phobia or perceived illness. Most children are eager to confide in their parents, but some feel helpless in approaching them because they fear rejection or humiliation. They avoid asking for help from teachers because they don't want to be thought of as "dumb." Parents and teachers can help by making statements of understanding and opening the way for dealing with children's concerns. An example: "It seems to me that you have been worried about something. Are you having some problems at school? It's okay to talk about how you feel. If I were in your place, I would probably be feeling even worse than you. I want you to know that I love you and I always want to hear about your worries. You don't have to be afraid that I'll punish you. After all, one reason you're in school is to learn how to solve problems—not just math problems, but also personal problems. When you want to talk, I'll be ready to listen, but I'll wait until you're ready." Such statements usually bring relief and comfort to a worried child.

Stress Factors

Children who fear rejection by parents or teachers when they do not perform adequately may build up strong feelings of stress. This kind of stress works against them because emotions get in the way of thought processes needed to do schoolwork.

When children can't think clearly, their performance suffers. We all have similar situations. When emotions run too high, we lack rational thinking and give way to losing our focus. Parents who become overly anxious for the child during this stage may add to the child's level of stress. Then, we may be inclined to make such statements as: "You just need to study harder," and we increase the stress even more. Another approach might be, "It seems to me that you are feeling pretty awful about something. When I feel like that, I can't think straight. Is there something you want to talk about? Maybe I can help." Confident parents are able to provide a calm and matter-of-fact approach to facing stressful situations. Children generally respond positively when they don't feel threatened.

Some children feel like they are letting their parents down when they cannot perform at the highest expectations. But when parents assure their children they expect them to do their best, but without ridicule, children generally let go of the stress. When they feel their parents' support, they are more willing to face their school challenges.

Sibling jealousy is strong during this stage, especially when there is a younger sibling still at home with the parent. School-age children often find ingenious ways to capture the attention of parents. This is a time when parents are wise to help by acknowledging what the child is after. An example: "I think I know how you must feel. It seems that every time you need me to help you with a special project, I am busy with your baby brother. There must be times when you wish you didn't have this little brother so we could spend more time together." These kinds of statements help latency children know that parents understand how they feel. Then, they are more open to moving toward a solution rather than resentment.

A Time for Support and Encouragement

While latency is generally viewed as the calm period of childhood, we can nevertheless see why many children still need lots of support and encouragement. They count on their parents for emotional stability and to be there for them when they bring home their wonders and their woes.

Together Forever
We were just a couple of kids.
Rebels without a cause.
Best friends forever.
Together till the end.
Without even a pause.
Always together.
Even in trouble.
I knew what she was thinking,
And she the same for me.
I was like her double.
We had a friendship like no other.

We had been through everything.
Trials and tribulations.
That kept us strong.
Our engine was without a ding.
We made a pact
That we'd always be together.
And that our friendship would never fray.
It's been so long.
I wonder what she's doing today.
—Kristin G. Wood, Age 12

Killer Whale Fable

One day in the Antarctic Ocean, there was a huge killer whale named Mischief. Mischief was a whale that always got lost. One day, a man on a ship that was carrying oil hit an iceberg. The oil spilled into the Antarctic Ocean. The oil does not mix with the water. It stayed and became stickier. Then it formed greasy tar balls. Mischief was curious about the greasy tar balls. He went closer to them. They looked strange to him.

Mischief smelled them. They smelled like danger to him. He got away in a moment, but he stayed to watch the oil. He kept on moving toward it slowly. A girl was watching Mischief from the shore. She knew that the whale was in danger because she had studied about oil spills in her class. So she hurried to her rowboat. She had brought some loud music to scare Mischief away from the oil. It worked! The girl cheered. Now, Mischief was out of danger. He swam back to his family. Someone was watching the girl from the shore. They told the captain. The captain gave her a medal and a paper scroll for saving an endangered animal.

—Courtney L. Crawford

Adolescent Ascendants

Up, up, and away! Not like a hot-air balloon, but more like a rocket to the moon—perceptions of adolescent ascenders abound wherever a teenager resides. Keeping up with them means securing your fast-lane running shoes and adjusting your "epistemological eyeglasses" because these humanoids are entering a whole new way of life!

Adolescence, the period between puberty and physical maturity, may be the stage that gives parents greater concern than any other. While there are some parents who enjoy the teenage years more than earlier periods, many are frustrated and besieged with daily challenges.

The smarter they are, the greater the challenges for those around them. As teenagers, they are ingenious at seeking their independence from parental authority. At this stage, they tend to vacillate between being oppositional or defiant, and being in great need of parental support. Their cycle of opposition hasn't been this strong since toddlerhood!

Perhaps adolescence is such a difficult period because parents expect mature behaviors on the one hand and, yet expect their teenagers to be compliant on the other. Teenagers often feel "caught" in a dilemma between independence and compliance. As one sixteen-year-old said, "I'm old enough to drive, and I have my license, but I still have to ask permission to carry the car keys. Don't they trust me?"

A Period of Transition

This period of major transitional change away from childhood begins with a spurt of growth and is impelled by hormonal changes until the stage of young adulthood. Major tasks for the adolescent during the period from about age thirteen to nineteen years include achieving:

- A sense of responsibility
- Self-sufficiency
- A relatively mature body
- Adult perspectives
- Relationships, dating, and interchanges with peers

Growth Spurts

The adolescent's gradual increase in size and weight that had prevailed since age two abruptly shifts into high gear. Children generally gain about four to six pounds a year until about age ten to twelve, just before the onset of puberty. Then, during their teens, girls gain about eleven pounds and grow three to four inches a year, and boys gain about fourteen pounds and grow four or five inches a year. These growth spurts continue for the next five to six years, or throughout the adolescent stage. Two factors about this upsurge influence the appearance and behavior of adolescents:

- Girls mature up to two years earlier than boys.
- There is considerable variation among individuals in the time of onset of the spurt in growth.

Critical Period of Development
Passage through adolescence forms a critical period. Successful integration, or a mature sense of self with a mature body, depends on a reasonably successful passage through all prior stages. Parents may be caught off guard to see their teenagers changing so rapidly.

Biological Changes Bring Apprehension
Adolescents may be viewed as "growing away from childhood." This begins when the calm of latency is upset by biological changes that usher in puberty. Secondary sexual characteristics start to emerge, and the teen feels separated, or estranged, from his or her own body. Upsurges of sexual feelings intervene in fantasy, dreams, thoughts, and behavior to change perceptions about one's self. There's a sense of *I'm not the same anymore. I wonder if anyone will still like me.*

Increased intellectual capacity helps the adolescent deal with the "biological ripening." For example, the teenager has to find appropriate ways to redirect sexual impulses and behave more like an adult than a child. This gets to be frustrating at times, especially when parents expect the adolescent to be mature one minute, yet follow parental dictates the next.

Psychological Sense of Self
Both the move toward independence from the family and the control and redirection of sexual impulses require a kind of reorganization of one's sense of self. The major task is to clarify and strengthen one's own *gender identity*.

- Boys must overcome dependency upon their mothers.
- Girls must become motivated to find satisfaction and attachments outside the family.

Conflicts with Parents

Adaptations have to be made by both parents and adolescents. This often brings turmoil. Conflict arises, and there are squabbles over parental expectations and adolescent perceptions.

Emotional problems often emerge as anxieties arise over issues of independence. The adolescent has to continually sort out what is happening and come to grips with how and where life will be directed. Failure to resolve one's own internal conflict may bring further difficulties, such as:

- Withdrawing from social participation
- Refusing to live according to cultural and social expectations
- Retreating into fantasy guided by delusion rather than reality
- Turning away from restrictions of social living and seeking to live outside the law

Three Overlapping Stages of Adolescence

1. **Early adolescence.** This prepubertal stage is when a spurt in growth brings about major developmental changes. Yet many patterns of childhood continue, and many adolescents remain in monosexual groups. The home is still very much the center of life.

   This is a time when the child is provoked toward breaking attachments to parents. We might say a *metamorphosis* brings about a new and definitive physical difference between the sexes. At the same time, there is also an increase in the attraction between them. This means both boys and girls have to search for a new type of intimacy and gratification in order to find happiness and motivation. Bonding changes from closeness to peers of the same sex to allurements between the sexes.

2. **Middle adolescence.** This period sets in when movement toward the opposite sex actually breaks up peer groupings. This is a pivotal time of life when the youth turns away from the family that has

formed the center of his or her existence for the first thirteen to fifteen years.

- **A period of revolt and conformity.** Revolt from parental and adult dictates casts the teen in a role of challenge and defiance. Conformity to peer group standards and loyalties becomes the norm. This often takes parents by surprise. They may not be ready for such a shift in behavior.

- **Overcoming sexual repression.** Adolescents are caught up in exploring their own sexual feelings. They are more concerned with breaking through inhibitions and testing their own limits than with pursuing intimacy. Love and sex may be kept quite separate in the mind of the adolescent at this stage. The urgency of sexual impulses is strange and can be frightening to the adolescent. To make things worse, parents cannot help their children much in managing or satisfying their sexual needs. While parents can prepare, discuss, and advise, a great deal must remain intensely personal. This is especially sensitive for both the adolescents and the parents because it involves separating and differentiating from one another.

  To complicate this developmental scene, many parents feel rejected by their teenagers who don't want to talk with them about personal problems. This is often a time when they turn to peers or other detached adults. They want to share their feelings, but they often think their parents "just won't understand." Whether perceived or real, these ideas create distance between teenagers and their parents. Perhaps this is a natural way in which adolescents begin the move toward mature independence.

- **Overcoming family dependency.** This is a time of marked ambivalence. Mood swings are further beset by wanting one's parents and wanting to be rid of them. Even so, the adolescent internalizes standards and values established by parents in family life. Experiences within the family during the years before adolescence have a deep-seated impact on the adolescent, even though parents may wonder at times whether all is lost.

- **Conscience orientation must be strengthened.** In order to become suited for adult, rather than childhood, behavior, the adolescent must develop mutual respect and make judgments that are in the best interest of others as well as himself or herself. Parents must be willing to maintain limits that are still necessary and stand firm in helping their children face consequences of misbehaviors. For example, when a teenager violates the limits regarding the use of the car, then discussion about consequences is a must. If this means taking away the keys for a week, then parents have to be firm and follow through. Is there any wonder that parents and adolescents have such tough times?

3. **Late adolescence.** By the last couple of years of adolescence, the concern is with real tasks of coming to grips with one's future. While some adolescents reach this stage as late as eighteen or nineteen, others mature earlier. So again, parents have to be flexible. This is especially important when there are two or more siblings in the adolescent stage at the same time.

   Reorganization of one's *identity* comes to completion as the adolescent reaches the end of this stage. Now that parent and child are clearly delineated one from the other, guidance may be welcomed. Education and career plans are uppermost. In many cases, marital choices bring a clearer sense of self and strengthen capacities for intimacy.

   - **A sense of interdependence grows out of independence.** Now the older adolescent engages in mutual relationships, making judgments and decisions that impact others as well as himself or herself. The adolescent moves beyond a self-centered perspective of the world. During this later stage, one begins to see himself or herself moving through a complex world and a maze of people rather than having others pass through his or her world. There is now greater appreciation and respect for the viewpoints of others, including parents.
   - **Overcoming the identity crisis** sets a theme of "Who am I?" The individual realizes that if he does not make decisions, the passage of time will make them for him.

- **A period of moratorium** allows for turmoil and despair while accepting responsibility for independent choices and their consequences. This is time for exploration without "playing for keeps." Engagements for marriage may be broken, changes in a choice of college or university may occur, and traveling or working before beginning college may be a consideration. Some adolescents may flee from their familiar surroundings and leave home or college, as if distance will resolve their problems. The change may, in fact, provide a respite during which one gains additional experience. This is a time to broaden one's viewpoint while increasing emotional maturity, both of which are needed to find direction and a sense of purpose.

- **Intimacy is attained.** Intimacy comes when an individual is capable of balancing giving and receiving, and can seek to satisfy another rather than simply seeking self-fulfillment and achievement. The older adolescent begins to see parents as individuals with lives of their own. Suddenly, parents have become intelligent again!

Best Friends . . .

Best friends stick together through thick and thin and the good and bad . . .

Best friends know each other's feelings, hopes, and dreams, and talk about problems.

Best friends can always count on the other for moral support and advice at hard times.

Best friends keep each other sane and look out for each other and look out for the other's feelings.

If this is all true, then someone tell me, please, what to do when she turns to alcohol and nicotine for help instead of me?

Her attitude and personality changed, and it's like I'm talking to a totally different person than before. Sometimes I feel like I'm the person she just has to ignore...

Someone tell me, please, do I tell anyone my concerns? Or do I just sit back and pray while she slowly drifts away?

I know I'm not responsible, but God, there must be something
I can do. Something has got to happen, or it seems like our
friendship is through . . .

I feel as though I'm alone and no one else cares. I feel as though I
am trying to move a mountain with my bare hands.

Two's company, and three's a crowd. That's what I feel right now.
I'm sorry if I'm the one who really cares, but dammit, someone
sure as hell better, or else . . .

I know that someday, any day too soon, he's going to break her
heart, and oh, God, she'll completely fall apart . . .

I know I just can't sit back and watch as her life deteriorates, but
her lessons can only be learned from futuristic mistakes.

—Anonymous Teenager

CHAPTER 4

Brain Works:
How Children Learn

Domains of Intelligence

D id you know that your child has not one or two intelligences, but eight? More than three decades of research at Harvard University, by Dr. Howard Gardner and his colleagues, provides widespread and cross-cultural evidence that a set of eight domains of intelligence begins to emerge at birth.

1. **Logical-mathematical**—the application of logic and abstract reasoning to solve problems and to create new ideas. Examples are scientists, computer technologists, mathematicians, managers, and economists.
2. **Language**—the ability to use verbal symbols and speech to express thoughts, feelings, and perceptions. Examples are poets, writers, speakers, linguists, and actors.

3. **Musical**—sensitivity to rhythm, pitch, sound, and tone to reflect and communicate feelings and thoughts. Examples are composers, musicians, dancers, and singers.

4. **Bodily-kinesthetic**—mastery of body movements and sensitivity of the body in its relationship to space, other people, and objects. Examples are performing artists, athletes, martial artists, and physical therapists.

5. **Spatial**—the ability to use the senses and perception in relationship to line and direction, movement patterns, design, and multidimensional representations. Examples are pilots, architects, astronauts, artists, designers, engineers, and astronomers.

6. **Intrapersonal**—awareness of self and the ability to apply introspective thought. Examples are writers, scientists, inventors, and philosophers.

7. **Interpersonal**—awareness of others and the relationship of oneself to them. Examples are leaders, teachers, performers, politicians, statesmen, and consultants.

8. **Naturalist**—awareness of and sensitivity to certain features of the environment, such as how things grow and develop in and on the earth. Examples are horticulturists, farmers, gardeners, florists, food scientists, artists, entomologists, veterinarians, and forestry and wildlife specialists.

Each child is born with a natural blend of these intelligences. What goes on at home and in everyday life will influence how these intelligences unfold. Some children are more inclined to excel in one or two domains, while others may function at a high or moderate level in several, or even in all of them. You may have a mathematical genius who cares little about athletics, or a musician who wants nothing to do with math. You may be challenged by a child who seems to excel in all domains. Qualities of genius in one or more of these intelligences may become obvious early in a child's life. Others may take years to master. Depending on how they are valued and pursued, some of these domains require more time to develop than others. For example, with logical-mathematical intelligence, it may be up to twenty years before a person has sufficient biological maturity and experience to master certain math concepts. On the other hand, musical intelligence appears to be one of the earliest to develop in the human. Some children may be recognized as precocious in music as early as age four or five years.

Your child's success in school and life depends on opportunities to develop these domains in natural, yet stimulating, ways. While we can separate these domains to discuss them, we must be aware that they are all working together within each person. Some domains may be more profoundly obvious than others, yet they all form a whole.

The human brain continues to baffle its user. Will we ever catch up with the potential produced beneath the skull, or will it continue to spiral just beyond our reach?

How Children Learn

Every dawning day in a child's life is filled with thrilling challenges to master the tasks of becoming more intelligent. One of the greatest joys of parenthood is watching a child leap forward in learning. Children learn in a variety of ways, but there are a few that are more obvious and powerful than others.

1. **Children learn from experience.** As they get involved, they actively engage in learning. Whether in the classroom or "on the street," children carry with them a "gold mine" of potential for success. Children who are successful in school achievement are usually those who experienced close and loving relationships with their parents the first three years of life. A solid emotional base leaves children enthusiastic and free to learn.

2. **Children learn from models.** Children are profoundly influenced by what they experience in the midst of others who serve as models. Parents are their children's most influential teachers. Teachers and other adults have a major impact on how children perceive themselves and the world around them. They also learn from their peers. Children whose friends are good students generally do better in school. By the same token, they may "con" each other into mischief. Since they have not yet fully developed their conscience orientations, children are unable to consistently make good judgments about what to do. Some models are

examples of acceptable behavior, while others serve as examples of less desirable behavior. As children experience the behavior of others, they begin to imitate and model similar behaviors. Parents who live in a way that demonstrates responsibility for their own lives will see benefits reflected by their children's behavior. Children who experience love, kindness, and respect will emulate these virtues.

Even infants and toddlers are sensitive to what goes on around them. When a mother is depressed or not feeling well, the child seems to take on some of the mother's feelings. A child may express sensitivity to the parent's feelings through fussy behavior or doing things to get the mother's attention.

By using their same inner resources, children can as easily emulate destructive aggression and disrespect when daily examples are filled with these less desirable behaviors. For example, some children who appear to be "hyperactive" may be mirroring the frenetic and stressed behaviors of their parents. Fortunately, when parents have their own lives in balance, their children are generally settled, too.

3. **Children learn by watching and asking questions.** Your children, during the early years of life, learn quickly by following adults around, watching and talking with them about what they are doing. One four-year-old whose father is a computer programmer was "hanging around" while his dad was working on a computer at the local school. The child kept asking his dad such questions as, "What are you doing?" His dad would reply, "I'm taking this modem out of the system." The child would say, "What's a modem?" His dad would tell him, and the child would reply by saying, "I know what that is." Then he would ask another question and another. Each time, his father talked with him as if he could understand everything. While it was obvious the child could not always understand, he nevertheless felt important. He probably will learn more about computers from his dad than by reading books about them. When he gets to middle or high school, computer science will be a breeze for him because of the emotional tie to his dad and to the good times they shared.

4. **Children learn by listening to others.** They learn when they hear parents talking, other children playing, and other adults in conversation. Parents may be unaware that children are listening and learning, especially when they seem to be preoccupied.

A five-year-old was heard cursing and using profanity. His mother had warned him several times about this being unacceptable behavior. She said the next time she heard him cursing, she would have to wash his mouth out with soap. So of course, it happened, and she took him into the bathroom and washed his mouth out with soap. He was willing, without a fuss, to face this consequence, but when she finished, he looked at her and said with great sincerity "Mom, do you really think this will help?"

This young boy learned slang words and phrases from the men who worked on their farm. He followed examples they set in his daily environment.

A father reported that his three-year-old son was playing with his hammering set when he began to spout a series of obscenities. His dad quickly intervened and said, "You know you are not supposed to say those words," to which his son replied, "Oh, yes, that's what you have to say when you hit your thumb with the hammer." The parents recalled that recently they had workmen doing some repair work on their house, and their child enjoyed following them around. He quickly learned their pejoratives.

Stages of Learning

All children go through similar stages of learning, yet each child progresses at an individual rate and in a unique way. These stages are predictable, making it possible for us to observe a child's progress.

The great Swiss psychologist Jean Piaget, by getting down on the floor and playing with children, discovered how children learn. For more than fifty years, he talked with children, watched, listened, and studied their behaviors. Piaget was interested in children's logic and how it influenced their thinking as they progressed in their development. He identified the following stages of learning.

1. **Infant-parent stage (sensorimotor)**
   (Birth to about two years)

   The child learns primarily through the body and the senses while interacting with the parent and other caregivers. At this stage, the baby actually thinks "through the parent" or other people. That is, the child's actions are in relation to others. For example, when babies are hungry, they cry, and *someone* comes to help them. When they want to play, they reach out to *others*.

   Intelligence appears through actions that are governed by body sensations of movements, sights, sounds, touch, smell, taste, and eye contact. *Feelings* are a major part of learning at this stage. These feelings and sensations register in the brain, making connections with previous ones until new patterns form.

   Babies have the ability to take action as well as to respond. That is, they do something, such as touch a ball and see it roll. Even though this action may be incidental, the baby feels excited about the movement and giggles. Then the baby may reach out and attempt to get the ball—or entice someone else to do so. During seemingly simple play, babies are learning by using their bodies and by registering the actions in the brain. Every time the baby plays with a ball, new brain connections about balls are made, and the information is stored for later use with a vast majority of objects.

   Infants learn mostly through play and by interacting with caring parents and others who treat them with loving care. The physical contact and eye contact between the child and the adult have an impact on the child's brain. The human voice and certain kinds of music, such as classical baroque, also tend to stimulate the brain during this early stage of learning.

   Up to about the age of eight or nine months, it's difficult to spoil a child, but about this time, watch out! The reason is that an infant's memory is pretty well developed by nine months, and the child remembers what to do to get the parent's attention or to get what the child wants. Before this time, the infant is sensitive to the parent, but doesn't actually think about what to do.

Also at about nine months, the baby acquires *object permanence.* This means that the brain is developed enough for the child to hold in mind a memory of someone or something even when that person or object is out of sight. An example is when a mom leaves the room, and the baby cries out as if to say, "I don't want you to leave me!" Conversely, some babies don't cry when the parent leaves because this memory, or mind picture, is enough to comfort them. Another example is when a ball rolls under the furniture, and the baby crawls to the spot where it went out of sight.

Object permanence is a major milestone of intellectual development. This memory capacity tells us that the child is progressing normally. A couple of other behaviors come about as a result of object permanence. One is *stranger anxiety,* and the other, *separation anxiety.*

Stranger anxiety is when the baby knows and remembers the features and characteristics of parents and other familiar people. The baby makes quick mental comparisons when new people come into view. When a stranger or less familiar person appears, the baby may resist or even scream as if frightened. Actually, this is the child's way of saying, "I'm uncomfortable—you're not anyone I know." Some grandparents are offended when their grandchild resists them. They often make such remarks as, "This behavior didn't occur three months ago." Stranger anxiety is a contrast to what goes on for about the first six or seven months, when the baby is generally content to go to anyone who is kind and gentle and meets the baby's needs.

Separation anxiety is another mark of intelligence that occurs at about eleven to thirteen months. An example is when a child resists having to part with the parent. Since the child is attached more to the parent than to anyone else, the message is, "I'd rather be with you."

Because children are sensitive to the anxieties and feelings of their parents, they often respond in ways that reflect these feelings. A typical case is when a parent leaves the child in the care of someone else. The child is usually content if the parent leaves quickly after a hug and kiss and says while departing, "Have a great day! I'll see you later." There may be a short cry, but within minutes, the child is ready to play and get involved without the parent. On the other hand, when a parent lingers, saying good-bye several times, going back and forth for one more kiss, the child is likely to cry and carry on with tantrums or screaming. The child senses the parent's anxiety about leaving. The message the child interprets from the parent is something like: "I wish I didn't have to leave you. I worry about this place and how these people will care for you. This is not making me happy." The child is smart enough to play into this, crying and carrying on as if to reply: "Don't leave me! This is going to be terrible! I don't trust these people if you don't." Children may cry for half an hour or longer when parents linger.

Another mark of intelligence comes about fourteen to eighteen months of age. By this time, **the child can hold in mind images** of what to do with toys and with people. For example, toddlers can stack rings on a tower, nest cups, and work simple puzzles. Watch for two signs: The child begins to do unexpected things with toys and begins to manipulate adults.

The final leap in mental ability for this stage is called invention. The child formulates new ways of doing things. Examples of invention: Instead of pulling a toy around that has a string and wheels, the child dangles it and then begins to swing it. A child wants you to stop texting or using the phone, so he begins to climb up on "forbidden" furniture or pulls things off shelves, and if that doesn't work, he may throw a tantrum. When children succeed with these "tricks," they remember what to do next time to manipulate others.

2. **Prelogical stage (preoperational)**
   (Two to seven years)
   Seeing is believing. During this stage, children are highly intuitive and sensitive. They learn spontaneously, especially through play. They use their bodies, brains, and spirits in active pursuit of their natural curiosities.

Children learn best at this stage through *active involvement and communication* with others. By this time, children have language abilities that are beginning to dominate their mental character. Yet they are unable to think with adult logic, thus the term *preoperational,* or before the brain is biologically mature enough to function as a complete whole.

The brain is still maturing, but the child is unable to process complete mental operations, such as *conservation* and *reversibility.* Academic skills, such as writing, reading, and arithmetic, begin to take shape near the end of this period (about six or seven years of age) as the right and left hemispheres of the brain begin to interact effectively.

Characteristic thinking at this stage includes:

- A strong imagination and vivid fantasy.
- Enjoyment of role-playing and pretending.
- A high sensitivity to others and to one's own feelings.
- Intuitiveness.
- Unique logic that makes sense only to the child.
- A view of adults, especially parents, teachers, and grandparents, as omnipotent.
- A belief in magical thinking.
- Impulsiveness without regard to consequences.
- Interest in rules, rituals, and routines.

⚱ Example ⚱

Teacher: "How do you make water boil?"
Child: "You put eggs in it."

Children get a thrill from learning. That's why a three-year-old continues to explore in "off-limits" territory. Even when parents spank, scold, or explain, the child is drawn to new adventures filled with learning about his world. A four-year-old quickly learns to use an electronic or video game because the excitement of learning is stimulating. A five-year-old talks unceasingly because she is learning that language is another way to control the attention of others.

During this prelogical stage, we say children are *egocentric*, not yet capable of understanding another person's point of view. They tend to create their own logic, often tied to believing what they hear or see, or what it feels like to them. For example, a six-year-old asked his mother, "What color are the eyes in the back of your head? Why can't I see them?" This child had heard the common phrase that "mothers have eyes in the backs of their heads," and he thought that was why she seemed to know what he was doing in the backseat of the car. He did not grasp the logic of the rearview mirror or the comment about perceptive parents.

⚓ Example ⚓

Preschooler: "Why is Gramps in the hospital?"

Mom: "He had to have heart surgery."

Preschooler: "If he gets a new heart, will he still love the same people?"

⚓ Example ⚓

Teacher: "Can the sun be named the *moon?*"

Child: "No. Then it couldn't be light so I can play."

Teacher: "What does the moon do?"

Child: "It makes it dark at night."

Children at this stage are not yet able to complete a thought process and then return to its starting point. For example, children using play dough think that when you change the shape of an object, it also changes in size or amount. The child is unable to think through the entire process of shaping the play dough, then changing the shape, and then mentally reshaping the play dough into the original form. So the mental operation is only partially complete. Even when you talk with the child about the fact that no more play dough was added, or none was taken away, the prelogical child is convinced by what *appears* to be bigger or smaller.

At the beginning of this stage, the child thinks in relation to what is *external*, what is "out there." For example, dreams are thought by most three-year-olds to be in the bedroom, not too far "from my head." Gradually, the prelogical child combines external with *internal* sensitivity. Then dreams are thought to be partly external and partly internal, or "inside my head." Ask a preschooler where words come from, and you are likely to get an answer such as, "In my throat." If you ask where the words are before you say them, a likely response is, "In my bones."

Characteristic thinking includes **imagination and fantasy.** Children learn through role-playing and pretending. They use intuition and sensitivity to create their own logic. They are influenced mainly by what they see and do at the moment: "The place is here, the time is now, and the center—of the universe—is me." Adults, especially parents, are viewed as omnipotent, all-knowing, and all-powerful.

⚓ Example ⚓

Adult: "Is the table alive?"

Child: "No, silly."

Adult: "If I hit it, would it feel it?"

Child: "No, it's not a person."

Adult: "If I hit it so hard it broke all to pieces, would it feel that?"

Child: "Yes, it would feel that."

Play is the child's pathway to learning during this stage. Play offers freedom to use the body, senses, and the mind to practice skills that will later be used in school and in everyday life. Children often calm themselves after an ordeal. They learn to negotiate with one another, solve problems, and share time and toys. Children also use play to express their feelings and thoughts. They learn through fantasy and pretending. Parents who think children aren't learning if they are playing are mistaken. Children develop two abilities through play that will be useful throughout their school years and in everyday life; one is *discovery*, and the other is *invention*.

⚓ Example ⚓

A four-year-old and her aunt were talking about some of the wonders of nature—the moon, clouds, wind—when the aunt asked her niece, "Where are the stars during the day?" The child replied, "They go on the flags, of course."

Parents and teachers help set the tone for children's play. When children feel free to exercise their imaginations, their intuitions, and their ideas, they develop patterns for thinking. On the other hand, when children feel restricted or pressured, they tend to close themselves off and lock their potential rather than express it.

Children who play with ease and spontaneity are emotionally and physically healthy, whereas those who cannot play tend to be troubled or in ill health. By giving children plenty of freedom to play—within the bounds of safety and respect—we make way for them to heal themselves when troubled and to express a full range of emotions. How children view themselves in their family and in the world is reflected in how they play.

- **Play serves as a bridge for making transitions from one stage of life to the next.** Play may be the most important way for children to develop the skills that enable them to deal with rapid changes bombarding them in a fast-paced and shrinking world.
- **Play sets the stage early in life for getting along with others.** Children develop patterns for negotiating, sharing, and problem solving as they play together.

Parents and teachers can help children develop their social skills by turning over to them the responsibility of learning to get along. Here are some examples:

- Avoid running interference when they get into difficulty. Open the door for communicating and talking about a situation, but let the children work through the problem or difficulty. Ask questions and acknowledge feelings to let them know you care, but resist the temptation to take over.
- Allow children to play out their differences and create solutions to their problems. Avoid intervening unless it is to prevent danger or hurting. Then, step in to give help without taking sides. Ask questions that will help them think through what they can do to get along with each other.
- Provide opportunities for children to play with a variety of friends. When they "tattle," or seek your help, encourage them to talk

with their friends, and let them know it's all right to get upset, but respect must be exercised.

- Set limits that help children learn respect for self, others, property, and nature. Follow through with consequences when they violate these limits of respect.
- Encourage children to share and cooperate without forcing a child to give in. Dramatic play helps children play out their feelings with dolls, costumes, and pretend characters. Outdoor play with balls, sand, water, and a variety of wheel toys allows children to express tension while having fun.

Parents who play with their young children, fostering love and trust, will enjoy watching them succeed later in school and in life. Children who are grounded in early mutual relationships grow up feeling free to learn and pursue academic interests.

---

3. **Logical-concrete stage (concrete operations)**
   (Seven to eleven years)

   Children master cognitive skills that require complete mental processes as long as they are bound to concrete, or direct, experience. The child may still think partly from within and partly through external, or outside, forces. For example, when you ask a child, "How do you know that?" you may get an answer such as, "I know it in my mind—and I read it in a book," or, "My dad told me, and I just know it is so."

   During this stage, children grasp the concepts of *conservation* and *reversibility*. For example, they know that when a play dough object is reshaped, it still contains the same amount of play dough. Unlike in the prelogical stage, now the child is able to mentally reverse the process and "see in the mind" that the object can be reshaped into its original form without adding or taking away any substance. This ability to complete a mental process makes it possible to perform academic tasks, such as math and problem solving, with success and enthusiasm. They can achieve adult logic and master language skills as long as they are tied to concrete ideas.

School becomes exciting. Between about age seven and eleven years, children gradually master thinking skills using whole-brain activity. This is the time when they enjoy working at a variety of school tasks. They like to please their teachers and their parents. They can cooperate in groups and work together on common goals. Study projects and teamwork are exciting and stimulating. They tend to learn best by interacting with one another. Friends are important and often are influenced by their peers.

Positive responses bring results. This is a critical time for developing a sense of self-importance and self-confidence. Consider how a child feels who comes home with a theme or book report, and the parent says, "I'd like to read your paper. May I see it?" Taking time to read it immediately gives the child the message, "I am interested in what you are doing and what your thoughts are." Contrast that with a child's feelings if the parent says, "Oh, just put your paper on the table. I'll read it as soon as I finish looking at the evening news." This child may feel a sense of diminished importance.

Feelings are important. Feelings at this stage are fragile, and children may cry when things go wrong. They also may develop unacceptable behaviors if that's the only way to get attention.

An example of just how smart children are at this concrete stage is the student who misbehaves in class to get attention because he can't succeed in academic tasks. If he can take the teacher's attention away from the lesson, he will not have to perform tasks that he thinks he can't do. And if that doesn't work, the child will not simply give up, but will try a variety of ways to bring importance to himself, even when it means succeeding at being the class clown—or the "best failure."

Peers are paramount. Not only are friends important at this stage, but children may attempt to exclude parents when peers are present. And they certainly don't want to share affection with their parents when their friends are with them. But as soon as they are alone with parents, they are quick to move in close for a hug and even a kiss.

This concrete stage of learning is the ideal time to help children develop sound study habits because they are open to guidance from parents and teachers. They are quick to form habits—good or bad—so take advantage, and begin early.

They do their best work when they have their own place to study. A desk or table, with a regular chair, out of the traffic of family members serves as an appropriate setting. Some children have their own rooms; others share or have space in the living area. Children need to be relieved of temptations, such as the radio, TV, telephone, or other electronics, including iPads and computers with Internet access. Parents are wise to simply place these distractions off-limits until homework and study are complete. In some cases, electronics are a part of the study process, and this is different from texting friends or interacting with others through Facebook.

After children get home from school or child care, they need about twenty minutes to snack and unwind before "hitting the books." They generally will do their best when they study for about twenty minutes at a time, take a short, five-minute break, and then get back to studying for another twenty minutes. While studying one subject, such as math, all other books and materials are best put aside, out of the way—even if they have to be placed on the floor under the desk or table. When a child forms consistent patterns, the brain will be ready to study as soon as the child walks into the study area and looks at the desk or work surface.

Some families are successful in making a ritual of study time. An example is when all the children, regardless of age, sit around the dining room table and study. They may ask questions, help one another, or simply work on their own. This becomes such a strong pattern that these children actually look forward to study time around the table. This approach to study habits requires the help of parents in excluding outside distractions.

Since families vary in their lifestyles and daily habits, each must generate patterns that fit their children's needs. But if study habits are going to be of value, children must have guidance and support from parents to enforce them.

4. Formal operations
(Eleven to sixteen years)

By the time children approach puberty, they are able to master the mental skills required to use abstract thinking to solve problems, to consider possibilities, and to think creatively. They are able to deal with a wide range of cognitive activities without reference to what is actual or concrete. They can synthesize; that is, transform thought and create new ideas that have useful and logical applications.

Problem-solving skills advance. From about age eleven to sixteen years, problem solving takes on a new dimension. The child is able to consider a broad range of hypotheses, possibilities, and expected outcomes.

Creative, or divergent, thinking is accomplished without reference to what is concrete or actual. This is a time when a child can hold one idea in mind while considering what will happen if certain conditions or actions occur. Then a comparison can be made between options.

The child is smart enough now to learn from a variety of experiences and from the thinking of others. But more than this, the child also can synthesize, or form new ideas, based on his own thinking about existing theories or concepts.

Here are two examples of how children think—first, concretely, and then formally:

"My teacher became so upset that he threw his pen on the floor and stomped out of the room, leaving the students alone to figure out how to set up the model spacecraft."

"My teacher was unable to maintain his composure as he withdrew in order to force the students to solve the problem of organizing the approach to engineering the deployment of a spacecraft simulator."

While both statements send essentially the same message, the first is easily understood by the concrete thinker, while the second one requires formal, or abstract, thinking.

Some students continue to learn by using concrete examples, while others tend to enjoy abstractions. In either case, most children by the age of twelve or thirteen are capable of formal, or abstract, thinking.

They can interpret myths and symbols. Another example of this advanced form of thinking is how children interpret myths and symbols. You can say to a teenager, "When you conquer the monster within you, you will have an ally for life." The formal thinker knows that this statement can be interpreted to mean, "When you find a way to use the unexpressed energy within you, which may otherwise turn to fear or anger, you will be able to get things done with less effort or frustration." The younger, or concrete, thinker might interpret this to be an imaginary monster that wants to be helpful, but the child may not be able to interpret the greater message.

Learning Styles

To capitalize on the fact that children are so smart, we need to become familiar with how they learn. A person's learning, or thinking, style is a combination of how the brain processes what a person experiences and feels. The brain takes in stimuli, or impressions, through the senses— hearing, seeing, feeling, tasting, and smelling. Specific brain patterns then convert the stimuli into meaningful information. Think of a television set or an iPad. We know that the air carries images and sounds in the form of impulses, or radio waves. These impulses are converted in the TV set or iPad to electrical signals, which, in turn, reflect pictures and sounds that we can see and hear. In a similar way, a person gets an impression of an experience, and the brain converts it into meaning.

Learning styles can be observed as early as infancy. As children grow and develop, we notice that some are more alert to what they *see*, while others pay more attention to what they *hear*. Many like to *touch* everything, and still others tend to *move* about in order to learn. These patterns, or learning styles, emerge as children play and interact with others.

The styles by which children process experience vary among individuals. Virginia Satir, world-renowned for her work in communication skills, identified basic styles that are generally common among children and adults. As you play or interact with your child, which of these four basic learning styles seems more prominent?

- **Visual.** Life derives much of its meaning from how things appear. Visual children respond to adult body language and facial expressions. They enjoy activities that involve bright colors, moving objects, picture games, and eye-to-hand tasks. Their speech reflects this style through such phrases as "Do you see what I mean?" "Let me show you what I'm talking about," and "It looks to me like . . . ." While the brain takes in what the child hears or feels, this input is converted into visual patterns that make it easy for the child to understand. When communicating, visual learners like to look at people's faces, especially their eyes.

- **Auditory.** Children with this style seem to pay more attention to what they hear than to what they see or feel. They enjoy listening to stories, CDs, podcasts, and people's voices. They may be found singing and chanting to themselves while studying or doing things. They are quick to respond to what is said and to voice tone, regardless of body language or facial expressions. Their phrases contain such auditory signals as "Do you *hear* what I mean?" "It *sounds* to me like you . . . ." Auditory learners usually can sit still, listen, and follow verbal directions. What they see and feel is converted by the brain into auditory signals for ease in learning. Eye movements generally will be from side to side, either left to right or right to left.

- **Kinesthetic.** Actions speak louder than words. Body movements are important. Children like to make physical contact with others and move about while playing and learning. Phrases may include such words as "I *feel* like *doing* . . . ." "Let me *hold* it." What is heard or seen is converted by the brain into kinesthetic patterns for processing. This learning mode is quite common, and those who have this pattern enjoy studying and playing with others. They like to take breaks while studying so they can move around. They shift body positions often.

- **Visual-kinesthetic.** Some children learn by active involvement that brings together their use of sight and body movements. These children respond readily to adults who use lots of body language and facial expressions. They want to move through space to get to something that catches their eye. They will go over, under, around, or through to get there. Students of this learning mode often are attracted to special interests, such as gymnastics, dance, painting, sculpture, race cars, swimming, and other visual-kinesthetic activities.

Some children are able to use all of these styles with great effectiveness. Others may tend to rely on one or two of these. When we know how a child learns, we can open avenues to activate that style. We also can provide experiences that help a child expand the possibilities for developing additional styles of learning.

> Lynx,
> You know the secret so very well in dreamtime and in the magic.
> But you will never tell.
> Observe to hold your tongue like the Sphinx.
> Powerful, yet silent, the medicine of the lynx.
> —Patrick Steele, Age 12

The Learning Atmosphere
School and home settings that provide suitable learning atmospheres will capture children's attention while encouraging them to learn according to their own styles.

Comfort Levels for Learning
In addition to the cognitive styles, certain conditions make a person more (or less) comfortable while learning. For example, a toddler who gets spanked every time she handles things on the coffee table may soon back away. She not only backs away from the coffee table; she backs away from

learning. It's too uncomfortable to explore and learn. On the other hand, a toddler who is free to explore things on the coffee table without fear of harsh consequences remains excited about learning. Why is the coffee table such an important place? Because it's in the middle of where others are, where others can see "what I am able to do." Of course, parents are wise to remove any breakable or valued items and replace them with objects of interest that are expendable.

Light and shade are considerations for comfort levels while learning. Some children gravitate toward the outdoors or sit by a window because they focus easier when they are in bright, natural light. Others prefer shady places or dim light, so they look for a nook or cranny. Visual and kinesthetic learners usually enjoy light and bright areas, especially outdoors. An auditory learner may be content to curl up in a private corner and read, or simply daydream.

The temperature is also a consideration. Some children are comfortable with a cool temperature, while others like it warmer. Some seem not to be affected by temperatures one way or the other. Some children are so focused on what they are doing that they are not aware of the temperature. Others can barely tolerate being too cool or too warm.

The time of day makes a difference, too. Some children are early risers; others are night owls. Some students are just getting started when parents are ready to go to bed.

Colors affect comfort, too. Large areas of color may bring more or less comfort to a person. Certain colors stimulate some children, while other colors seem to relax them. Generally, a neutral color, such as soft beige or a pastel, is comfortable for most children and adults. Children who tend to be active and on the move are often stimulated to distraction by too much bright color or flashy design.

The size of the group during play or study influences how children learn. Many children feel more comfortable with several friends around them; others prefer to be alone or with only one or two at a time. Some want to study alone.

Spaces may affect comfort. Many children like to move about and may need lots of open space. Others feel more secure in smaller areas. Generally, the younger the child, the smaller the space. Children need to feel safe, and too much open area can be frightening to an infant or young toddler. Cramped quarters, on the other hand, may inhibit some children. Simple, orderly areas usually offer the best environment for study and concentration.

Sound level is a consideration. Some children can tolerate a wide range of noise levels. Others want quiet surroundings. And there are some who prefer lots of sound. For most students, focus and concentration are enhanced by a quiet atmosphere, with no phones ringing, no TVs or radios playing, and no people walking in and out.

When you have a clear idea about the natural tendencies that mark your child's comfort level for learning, you can both appreciate and support your child's uniqueness. Parents and teachers who honor children's thinking styles and conditions for learning, contribute greatly to their overall growth experience.

Four Factors Influence Learning

Four factors influence a child's acquisition and application of knowledge. These same factors reflect the great potential in every child.

- **Biological maturation.** Brain cells and structures of the mind must be mature enough to handle certain mental processes.
- **Experience.** Children learn by interacting directly with people and objects in everyday life. They learn by their own, firsthand experience, then by what others experience.
- **Social transmission.** Parents and other significant people pass on values to children. They want to learn because it is important and valued by those closest to them.
- **Equilibration.** For learning to occur, children have to attain a "balance," or equilibrium, between what comes into their mental system and how they make use of it.

Cycles of Learning

Three cycles of learning occur: First, the child roughs in stimuli or information; second, he puts it in order or uses it in a way that makes sense for him; and third, he practices it and varies the information through a wide range of experiences and applications.

Relational Concepts

During infancy and the preschool years, children develop four relational concepts. These are ideas about physical and logical aspects of the world that serve as a foundation for later academic tasks. While these relational concepts cannot be taught directly, children learn them through play and daily activities. These concepts are:

- **Classification.** This is the process of organizing objects or ideas according to similar properties or characteristics. Classification is necessary for learning to write and read; an "a" is different from a "b," and so on. Books stay on the bookshelf; blocks, on the block shelf; food, in the kitchen; and clothes, in the closet. Children first begin to classify by one concept at a time, such as by shape, color, and then size, but not all three at the same time. For example, a three-year-old who stacks rocks in one pile, leaves in another, and sticks in a third pile is classifying by shape. Gradually, they are able to classify subsets, such as identifying dogs by color, body build, and name of breed. Give a preschooler some felt or wooden shapes, such as triangles, squares, circles, and rectangles. While she plays, she will show her ability to classify. For example, she will put the circles together, and also the squares, the rectangles, and so on. If she also sorts these by color, you know that she has grasped more than one concept.

- **Seriation.** This is the process of ordering according to logic, such as by number, size, or weight. The easiest and first experiences in seriation are those that directly involve the child. An example is when helping a child get dressed. "*First,* you put on your underwear, *then* your clothes"; "*First,* you put on your socks, *then* your shoes." "*First,* you wash your hands, *then* you have your lunch."

   Five-year-old Patrick said he had cinnamon toast for breakfast. "First, Mom cooked the bread. Then she put butter on it when it was done. Then she put sugar on it. Then she put on cinnamon. Then I ate it!" By this account, we know that Patrick has the concept of seriation. Children also learn seriation by order of routines. They know what to expect next. Seriation helps children get ready for such school tasks as adding and subtracting, following written and spoken directions, and anticipating what to expect next. One five-year-old was asked, "Since your birthday is tomorrow, will you be six years old?" His answer was, "If that comes after five."

- **Spatial relationships.** These involve concepts or ideas about how objects fit into spaces and how lines form designs. Children learn that certain puzzle pieces fit together, that cars drive on a certain lane of the street, that round pegs fit into holes, and that coats hang on hangers. Later, these concepts serve as foundations for abstract thinking, such as learning geography and geometry; for designing highways, bridges, and buildings; or piloting spaceships, airplanes, and ocean liners.

- **Temporal relations.** The concept of passage of time is important for everyday living as well as for academic tasks. Children gradually learn about the idea that the younger siblings were born first because they are one year old. But to the young child, one is first because that's how they learned to count: 1-2-3-4-5-6. Gradually, they learn that a one-year-old was born last when compared with the three- and seven-year-old siblings. Many preschoolers can "tell time" by looking at the clock, yet they do not actually know what the hour means in relation to the day. Many children think of the passage of time in relation to themselves and what goes on in everyday life.

A five-year-old, traveling with his family, asked his mother, "How long till we get to California?" She said about three days. He said, "No, Mom, how long till we get there?" She said, "About twenty-four to thirty-six hours." He said, "No, Mom, how many sleeps till we get there?"

Children may not be able to understand the passage of time in such an abstract way, but they are smarter than you think. For example, many young children know when it's time for the parent to pick them up from child care. They sense it's about that time. Others begin to anticipate the parent's arrival when another child's parent arrives. Children often know when it's time to have a meal—and they are ready, or when it's time to get dressed for bed—and they resist!

Never underestimate the brilliance of your child—even before these relational concepts are in place. Children are smart enough to take detours to get what they are after. For example, a child senses that it's time to get dressed for child care. Parents are dressed and ready to go, siblings have their books and are ready for the bus, but one child dillydallies, wasting time and lingering at every turn. The child's mother starts saying, "It's time to go. Let's hurry; we don't want to be late. I have to get to work—" And the child gets slower and slower. In the mind of the child, *Why should I cooperate? It will only mean separation from Mom, separation from home, from my brothers and sisters, and my dog. I don't want to go.* While the child does not say these words, they probably represent how the child feels and how he is trying to reshape the reality of time to meet his own personal need and wishes. He may not understand temporal relations—the passage of time—as we do, but he understands separation from what's most important to him.

From Simple to Complex Thinking

Children progress from simple to complex thinking by levels of representation. Learning occurs on four levels and in order, as follows:

1. **Object level:** interaction with the real thing (a banana), to
2. **Index level:** experiencing something through one or more of the five senses (the smell of a banana), to
3. **Symbolic level:** recognition of two-dimensional representations of the real thing (a picture of a banana), and finally to
4. **Sign level:** words and numbers that are abstract representations of what is real (the written or printed number and word "2 bananas").

The "Learning Loop"

The learning loop is a concept based on how the brain connects and stores new information that is taken in. Whether the child is in the classroom or at play, information that is experienced is actively processed, and new connections are made. A loop of learning occurs as the child sees, hears, notes, and acts on new information. Each of these processes "connects" the same information in a different way. So the child has an **integrated approach** to grasping the idea or concept being considered.

For example, in a class discussion about the human brain, the student first *sees* what the teacher presents in chart form. This visual process sets the learning loop in motion as the student builds a mind-picture of the human brain. The student then *hears* what is said about the brain, and the auditory process makes another connection. As the student *takes notes or draws* diagrams of the brain, a visual-kinesthetic connection continues the loop. Then students *talk and ask questions*, interacting with one another and the teacher. This action makes the connections of information even stronger. Finally, the student *performs* by expressing his or her understanding or by responding on a quiz. Each of these processes strengthens the student's understanding and application of information about the human brain—or whatever subject is under study.

How to Activate the Learning Loop

Parents and teachers can encourage five dynamics that make brain connections for increasing memory and understanding:

- **Visual.** Present an idea or new material in visual form.
- **Auditory.** Talk about it so the child hears it.
- **Notation.** Have the child write, take notes, or draw about it.
- **Action.** Make way for the child to do something with the information through such action as discussions, projects, and questions.
- **Expression.** Provide opportunities for the child to talk about it and demonstrate an application of understanding.

Mind-Charting and Doodling

Mind-Charting for Memory and Understanding

Taking notes by drawing mind-charts, instead of writing words in outline form, also helps to activate the memory. These charts give just enough information by using key words and lines to make connections of thought, or *mind linkages*. The child begins to make connections between the ideas already in the memory and the new information being discussed in class.

Doodling for Concentration and Comprehension

We may think the child is paying no attention when doodling or scribbling in the margins of a notebook while studying or listening in class. But this is a natural way for the brain and body to help the child focus. While drawing squiggles or designs, the right hemisphere helps the child visualize or concentrate on what is being discussed.

Some children use a combination of doodling, mind-charting, and outlining. The child's style of learning will influence patterns for building unique learning skills.

Reading Readiness

Reading is a skill. Many children learn to read by "sight," or by connecting pictures with words and memorizing them. Some children can *sound out* the words because they have memorized the alphabet and are beginning to connect, or "string," sounds together to form words. While a child is doing this, there is little comprehension or actual understanding of the concepts within the reading material. While these exercises are preparation for reading with comprehension, children still need time to mature and develop mental structures.

When we wait until children are about seven years old, we find they usually learn to read in about two weeks. By this time, the two hemispheres of the brain and the corpus callosum, which connects them, are mature enough for the child to read and understand at the same time. When the brain is mature enough and when they are motivated and psychologically ready, children are on their way to success with reading.

Children who show an interest in reading need opportunities to begin by using their natural approach to the task. By watching them and being there with them, we can usually determine their style. Some children are more interested in the pictures than the words. Some like the sound of words and enjoy sounding out new words. Some children prefer to write their own words, spelling them according to their understanding. Expectations for early reading have little advantage for the child. To the contrary, this may do something to prevent the child from enjoying reading. Children have ways to protect themselves from a sense of defeat or failure. Or, they may simply view themselves as "not very smart." The early push to read may actually push the child *away* from books.

Some children do learn to read early, even by age four or five. Primarily, this means that maturation of the brain is a little earlier than usual. The question of concern is, Does the child understand what he or she is reading?

Preparing your child for school success begins in the first few months and years of life. Your child has the capacity to make brain connections for learning to read years before letters, words, and sentences are recognized.

How can you be sure your child will develop an interest in reading? By doing three simple activities, your child will reach for books and love to read throughout life. This works best when you start during your baby's first months of life, but it's not too late during the preschool years.

1. Snuggle your baby in your lap, and read a book out loud. This can be a baby's book, or it can be one of *your* books or magazines. Do this at least five minutes each day.
2. Continue to snuggle your toddler in your lap while reading books, especially those with big pages and lots of pictures. Poems and nursery rhymes are as good as stories.
3. As your child gets to be a preschooler, sit close together side by side. Read to your child at least once a day and again just before bedtime.

Reading to your child does two things. First, your snuggling and sitting close together brings feelings of comfort and love to your child. This makes powerful psychological connections between the mid-brain and the thinking brain. When your child sees books, wonderful feelings come rushing in and the child reaches for them. Books become symbols of the closeness between you. Second, your child holds the memory of your voice in mind and makes connections between words and mind-pictures. Stories and poems are easily remembered because they are connected with familiar and comforting feelings.

Helping Your Child Learn to Read

Watch for clues that tell you that your child is ready to learn to read. Here are some examples:

1. **The child will point to a sign, billboard, or line of words and say, "What does that say?"** There is a particular interest in words and how they fit together to "say" something. This statement is different from, "Let's read a story." The latter simply means the child enjoys being read to by you, and enjoys engaging in reading activities—a forerunner to becoming ready to read. When your child shows an interest, take time to talk about the words or phrase or sentence so the *idea* will have meaning for the child. Extend the thoughts. For example, if the child points to a billboard and asks, "What's that say?" Tell the child what it says, and carry it a step further. For example, say, "That says, 'Choose the bank that will serve you best.'" Now extend the idea with a statement such as, "Do you know what a bank is? A bank is . . . ." As you engage the child, the words take on meaning, and the next time the child sees the sign, all those thoughts will be activated, even though nothing may be spoken.

2. **The child has a clear concept of *right* and *left* direction.** The midline of the body is understood, with the right direction outward and the left direction outward. In addition, the child can place her left hand on your right shoulder and identify which hand and shoulder it is, respectively, right or left. What does this have to do with reading? In order to read, the child must be able to distinguish on which side of the line the circle is connected to form a "b," and the same is true for a "d," "p," "q," "g," etc. Also, the child must be able to know that following a line of words occurs from left to right, and at the end of the line of words one returns to the left margin to begin again. (This is one reason for writing or printing the child's name at the top left of paintings and other artwork the child has completed.)

3. **Spatial relationships are evident.** Children learn to read when they recognize letters and know how they fit together to form words. They have to know that each letter has a certain shape. For example, unless the child has spatial concepts, a "p" and a "q" may be confused, or a "d" and a "b" could be confused. The child also must be able to distinguish between those letters that are positioned above the baseline and those positioned below the baseline.

4. **Seriation is a concept that reflects the child's ability to make logical progressions.** The child gives indications of seriation through a variety of activities and play. You will recognize this aspect of "relational concepts" when the child knows that his name has a first and last section. You will observe the child lining up objects in graduated order according to size. Seriation makes it possible for the child to follow a sequence of letters and words to form sentences.

5. **The child is able to sit still for several minutes at a time and concentrate on one activity.** This attention span is essential for learning to read. As soon as a child becomes fidgety, you can be sure the power of concentration is lost, and attempting to read will become a chore and will discourage the excitement of learning. When the child is ready to read, there will be ease in sitting still, and you will notice an attentiveness to the process.

6. **The child initiates action.** Readiness to read is also signified by the child spontaneously making such statements as, "I know what that says; it says . . .," and the child is able to actually read or sound out the word. This is different from memorizing and recognizing single words.

Provide a relaxed atmosphere. Relax, and enjoy your child's enthusiasm for learning! Parents who are especially eager for their child to learn to read may communicate a sense of urgency. This can cause the child to become anxious and may result in avoidance of the task. Children want to succeed and please their parents, but when they are unsure of themselves, they will do anything to get out of the task.

Too much pressure on the *limbic system* lowers the efficiency of the neocortex. When this happens, the child momentarily loses capacity for thinking clearly—he is stifled. The greater the pressure, the less the capacity to think clearly.

Remain in the parent role. Give support and guidance without teaching. Avoid using specific methods, such as having a "reading lesson" or using flash cards. Children need to be able to come home to you and get the nurturing and support necessary to go back to school and face the "difficult" tasks. They need to enjoy being at home, basking in the luxury of having fun with parents. Of course, it's good to read together when both parent and child are in the mood. Take advantage of the opportunity to extend the learning process without taking on the teaching role. Use flash cards for fun when children are the initiators.

Building a Vocabulary

Building a vocabulary prepares children for reading. As they develop a storehouse of words that have meaning for them, the skill of reading will be easy and enjoyable for children.

Children enjoy words. They are stimulated to speak as they hear others talking and as they hear their own voices. Words become like magic to toddlers and preschoolers. They are quick to learn to use words to get what they want, even with two-word sentences. Children like unusual words, too. Favorites are such words as *triangle, dinosaur, rhombus,* and *purple.* Even before they can spell the words, children are able to use them correctly. Children expand their vocabularies as they talk and play with adults and children. Adults who read to children and talk with them about what they are doing help them expand their memories and enrich their vocabularies.

Speech and Language

Language provides a system by which children learn to use words to communicate through speech. The timetable by which they begin to talk in sentences varies greatly among children. Most are talking by the second or third year. While they may not start talking until two or three years of age, they are forming patterns for speech from the time they are born. During the infant and toddler years, it is important that children hear others talking. Ear infections and other hearing impairments during these early years may interfere with normal speech during the third and fourth years.

Children are capable of learning to understand and use more than one language. Some live in families with two distinct languages, yet they are able to grasp both. The earlier they are exposed to additional languages, the better. Most children will combine languages early on, but by the age of five or six, they sort out the differences.

Stuttering

A common reason children stutter is because they attempt to talk as fast as they think. Two-year-olds are still learning to develop a rhythm, or pattern, for speaking and often get "stuck" on a word. By three or four years, they get so excited they can't get the words to come out fast enough. Stuttering seems to be a natural way to give a child extra time to process the words and form sentences. Generally, stuttering gives way to smooth speech within a few weeks. When stuttering continues over a period of six or eight weeks, professional attention may be needed to rule out neurological or articulation problems.

What about Flash Cards?

Flash cards are generally less effective than using books when learning to read. Consider these three factors about flash cards:

1. Flash cards fragment thinking. The child memorizes a word with little opportunity to see it in context. This can result in choppy reading rather than smooth, flowing articulation.
2. Flash cards have little to offer in helping the child perceive reading as a skill that brings pleasure and meaning into life through a story or poem. There is little opportunity to relate the word on the card to reading.
3. Flash cards may have a subliminal intrusive effect on the brain. The words are stored in the memory but with little coding for later use. This may cause confusion or "jamming." How does the child decide which word to retrieve—to, two, or too; here or hear; their or there; know or no?

Use flash cards as a game when the child is interested. This gives freedom to "play" with words without pressures or expectations. This gives the child a sense of control and of leading the activity. This can bring the parent and child together in fun situations that build their relationship.

Children who are comfortable in early learning situations are able to handle academic tasks as long as they are within their range of abilities and skills. The first five years prepare the child for academics in the school years without the necessity of teaching the child directly.

Learning Problems

How do we know when a child has a real learning problem? Take the case of five-year-old Reneé, who has just been given an achievement test. The report indicated that she is somewhat delayed and should spend a second year in kindergarten. The test also reflected that Reneé was unable to copy certain geometric designs, could not match given words with pictures, and was unable to print her name. Her parents wanted to know whether this was a true learning disability, or if Reneé simply needed a little more time and experience to develop certain skills. How do the teachers or test-givers know whether Reneé has a real learning disability, or had a bad night, needs more time for brain maturation, was ill before the test, is coming down with a cold, or was simply frightened about having to perform strange tasks for a strange person? A more extensive evaluation is certainly called for in such situations if the child still has these problems at age six or seven.

Most children, at one time or another during their early years, will behave in ways that appear to reflect a learning problem. In many of these cases, however, children are actually going through natural periods of difficulty that will give way to more appropriate behaviors. How, then, can one determine what is a real problem and what is developmental? Even though this is not a simple matter, there are factors that can help parents and teachers sort through possibilities.

Many children are viewed as having "learning disabilities" and "behavior disorders." These terms, however, have serious implications and therefore require that we give serious attention to what they mean for children. Only a small percentage of children have disorders that result in a clinical diagnosis. Even so, some of the most intelligent children are faced with serious emotional or mental problems. In fact, some children are so smart they tend to become troubled because they sense the inconsistencies in their lives. They are keenly aware of what is going on around them, and they often carry the burdens of family and daily life with them. In an effort to protect their family members, some children are ingenious in hiding their own feelings. Too many strong feelings, such as fear and anger, when harbored within, can result in eruptions that are disabling for children.

Unfortunately, some children suffer from biologically based problems that are not easily resolved, regardless of how intelligent the children are. Some problems are inborn, and some result from birth defects or birth trauma.

Perhaps it is more important to know how to recognize disabilities and disorders, and help children face them, than to try to rationalize the disabilities' and disorders' existence or place blame for them. Of course, when a cause is determined, all possible effort can be made to help a child move forward toward resolution.

Learning Disabilities

Boys make up about 85 percent of learning disability referrals during the grade school years. Does this really mean that so many boys have learning disabilities early in life? No! What we are seeing here is that boys are *naturally* active and highly stimulated by what they see. They also move a lot. They see something of interest across the room, get up, and go after it. Their learning styles are often very visual and kinesthetic. They want to *see, touch, and examine* something in order to learn about it. They may not wait for permission, but instead will go around, over, and through whatever they have to in order to get there. In the school setting, this often presents problems. Girls, on the other hand, often have an advantage. They generally have a more active left-brain hemisphere during the first ten years of life, which makes them more *auditory.* They can sit still, *listen,* and follow directions easier than boys can. So, are we identifying boys as learning disabled when in reality they are actually active, whole-bodied learners who are excited and eager about exploring the world around them?

A small percentage of children suffer from *neurological,* or "brain-based," disabilities that interfere with their ability to learn. For example, a child may be unable to understand what he is reading because his brain cannot process the visual information correctly. It seems to be "scrambled." Another example is a child who has *dyslexia,* and therefore reverses letters and numbers, or cannot sort out the words and phrases for reading. The brain seems unable to distinguish the correct direction of letters and numbers. Dr. Povl Toussieng, a child psychiatrist with many years' experience working with children, called these conditions *problems of learning.*

On the other hand, he said, children with problems *about* learning experience external circumstances that influence their ability to learn.

Many of these children have negative ideas about themselves as a result of how they interpret their surroundings, such as family and school life. These self-perceptions often interfere with children's abilities to focus and concentrate on their schoolwork or home tasks.

Troubled children often have fears of failure, inadequacy, or rejection. Children who view the world as an unfriendly or fearful place often have problems about learning. While these children may be very capable of learning, their ideas about school and how adults view them is often distorted. For example, children who are physically abused may be so burdened with fear and worry that they cannot concentrate on their schoolwork. Even though many such children are intelligent, their emotions often block their ability to think clearly. These children generally need professional help to resolve their personal problems and clear the way for learning.

Examples of other situations that may interfere with learning are:

- Separation and divorce
- Serious illness or death of a family member
- Family violence
- Criminal offenses within the family
- Serious economic problems
- Moving from one location to another several times

What about Testing for School Placement?

Most children exhibit great variations in overall development until about age seven, when they begin to level off. By this time, they have crossed many expected milestones in language, social behavior, and thinking skills. The brain by this time also has matured enough to begin to process logical ideas presented in a school setting.

For the most part, it is safe to say that a child's ability will reflect both gradual and marked improvement between ages five and seven years. Test scores during this time may vary dramatically. Some brain research evidence suggests that during the fifth year of life, a child's left hemisphere is not as active as the right hemisphere. This being the case, we can expect many kindergartners to be using their bodies and their intuition for thinking and solving problems, rather than using their logic and analytical abilities.

Ask the school administrator or teacher to explain the purpose of testing your child. Clarify how the test results will be used. What will this mean for your child? Inquire until you are comfortable. Most school personnel are pleased to know that you are interested and will manage time for discussions about your concerns.

Holding a Child Back in School

How do you know when to hold a child back and repeat a grade in school? This is a difficult decision for parents and teachers.

Perhaps one of the greatest dilemmas parents face is holding a child back or pushing the child forward. Parents often feel a sense of failure when a teacher suggests holding a child back to repeat a grade or having a child wait a year before starting kindergarten.

There are both advantages and disadvantages in holding a child back in school, especially in kindergarten or first grade. Each child's situation is different, and parents are wise to consider both the short-term and long-term possibilities of their decisions.

Advantages

An extra year gives the child time to mature both physically and socially. The child grows in stature and may be viewed by classmates as "bigger and smarter." The extra time to increase social skills makes it possible to get along with peers and teachers with more emotional stability. The child masters the work with ease because it is familiar, or because the extra year's experience makes it easier to learn.

Disadvantages

The child likely will be bigger than peers and thereby see himself or herself as "falling behind" or "dumb" in comparison to the others. The child's self-image may suffer because he or she realizes that peers have moved on and "I'm still here"; therefore, "there's something wrong with me." The child may mature over the summer and actually be ready for the challenge of the next level, yet is held back from making normal progress. Parents expect the child to perform academically at a high rate of achievement, thus placing lots of pressure on the child to succeed. Parents may expect the child to be a leader when the child may not be motivated in that direction. The child may get bored and become a behavior problem because the repetition of academic tasks has little challenge.

I worked with a first-grade girl who had difficulty keeping up with her schoolwork when compared with her peers. The teacher suggested that the parents have the child repeat the first grade, giving many of the advantages listed above. Yet the child was as tall as many of her friends, she was well-behaved, she liked to attend school, and she was socially adapted to being a first-grader. She was, however, slower than her peers in finishing her work. When I observed her in the classroom, I saw that she was compliant, focused on her work, and seemed to enjoy doing it—but at a much slower pace than others. She obviously was on her own time frame and was unable to move ahead with the others.

While talking with this child in a private session, she told me that she was excited about being a second-grader the next year. She had been helping the kindergarten teacher with children's activities during her first-grade year. Her teacher thought she was very comfortable in the kindergarten setting with younger children, but the child perceived herself as their "other teacher." She had good motor skills, and her mental abilities appeared normal. Even though she progressed slower than others, she was an intelligent, competent girl, ready for the challenge of second grade.

Her parents later reported that she was receiving tutoring over the summer and she liked the tutor very much. This helped her gain self-confidence and increase skills, as she was not placed under too much pressure to work faster. She is now a successful second-grader and enjoys school, her teachers, and her friends.

When having to make the decision to retain or promote, the following questions may be helpful to both parents and teachers:

1. Is the child making obvious progress in each area of schoolwork regardless of the rate at which she works? For example, is the child able to spell more difficult words, and is her vocabulary growing? Is she showing progress in the use of numbers? Are reading skills taking shape in a way that indicates she is advancing? Does she show improvement in body control and eye-to-hand coordination?
2. Is the child able to talk about her comfort level in school? Are detected signs of fear or anxiety related to school, such as not

wanting to attend? Does the child make excuses to stay home, or is she becoming ill frequently without any real cause? Does she enjoy talking about school and her activities, both academic and social?

3. Does your child show an interest in reading for pleasure? Does he like to have you read to him, and does he want to read to you? Or does he avoid any reading opportunities?

4. Does your child seem to be happy most of the time? Is he spontaneous, does he get excited about playing with friends, and does he also enjoy doing things by himself?

5. Is your child curious, and does he get interested in a variety of pursuits—from playing games and building with blocks or Legos, to singing and pretending? Does he ask a lot of questions that indicate a desire to learn about the world around him?

While these questions don't provide the answers, they help sort out possible consequences of either retaining or promoting a child.

Children are smart and sense immediately what is going on when their placement is in question. Even though they may not say anything, they know that others are concerned about them. This knowledge and the feelings about how others view them tend to shape their own view, or self-image.

Children generally do what others expect of them. When we expect a child to fail, that usually will happen. When we expect a child to succeed, that also will happen. Why? Because once we, as adults, view a child a certain way, we tend to set the child up in our own minds to fulfill our prophecy. This, too, is natural, and as we become aware of our own expectations of a child, we can usually succeed in guiding that child toward realistic expectations. Parents and teachers who work out solutions together will be able to support the child's efforts and recognize accomplishments.

What are Normal Expectations for a Kindergartner?

When we know what to expect, we are better able to judge a child's readiness for kindergarten.

1. The child is excited about *starting kindergarten*. Many children go to a preschool or child care and have some notion of what to expect.

Otherwise, parents can take their children to visit kindergarten classes before enrolling.

2. The child is *naturally curious* and likes to make discoveries, finding out about new gadgets, toys, and other things—from birds to computers.

3. The child *can sit quietly for several minutes at a time* while engaging in listening activities, discussions, and individual tasks. This includes the ability to follow directions from an adult and carry out simple tasks that have a beginning and an ending. It is also natural for kindergartners to spontaneously get up and move about—many think easier while in motion at this stage.

4. The child shows an *interest in books*, but may not be able to read yet.

5. The child *enjoys listening* to stories read by the parent or teacher, and can respond about the characters and actions in the story in a way that reflects the ability to follow the story line.

6. The *skill of counting* is mastered, even though the child may not yet be able to add or subtract.

7. The child *can draw simple pictures and tell a story* that can be written down by the parent or teacher. The child enjoys seeing his or her picture and words posted.

8. *Social skills* are obviously progressing for getting along with others, sharing, taking turns, and working cooperatively on common goals in simple group projects.

9. *Self-confidence* is exhibited in most aspects of the child's involvement, so that the child reflects the notion "I can do it," or, "I want to work on it."

10. The child's *attention span is long enough to focus* on a simple task until it is finished—from two or three minutes to ten or fifteen minutes, depending on the nature of the activity. Artwork, music, dramatic play, and block-building usually capture a child's attention for longer periods than academic tasks during kindergarten.

11. The child *enjoys playing outdoors as well as indoors*, and shows interest in playing with others as well as alone.

12. The child *can take care of personal needs*, such as toileting, eating, grooming, and dressing, including combing hair.

What are Normal Expectations for a First-Grader?

1. The child *shows excitement about learning* and about going to school. The child looks forward to both classroom and outdoor activities.

2. The child *can tie own shoes* without any help.

3. The child *sits quietly for periods of up to fifteen minutes,* yet enjoys the opportunity to move about between sittings.

4. The child *likes to pursue such academic tasks* as writing, reading, and doing simple arithmetic, and can focus attention on these for several minutes at a time until a task is complete.

5. The child *reflects a broad vocabulary* of words and understands what they mean, and is consistently adding new words. The child likes to ask what certain words mean.

6. The child *asks lots of questions and can discover answers.* He or she likes to look up words in picture dictionaries, on electronic devices, and in reference books. The child enjoys going to the library.

7. The child is *attracted to class projects* as well as individual work. The child likes to work cooperatively with others as well as alone.

8. The child *can understand and follow rules.* He or she knows that rules are important and feels comfortable with them.

9. The child *views teachers as authority figures* and shows respect for them, using them as role models in forming their own ideas.

10. The child *enjoys engaging in discussions* centered around learning activities. He or she shows a high level of interest in pursuing knowledge and asks lots of questions as well as offers lots of answers.

11. The child *reflects social skills* as a basis for developing responsible behavior when given the guidance.

School Phobia

When a smart child does not want to go to school, it may have little to do with brainpower or intellectual ability. More than likely, the child is anxious about something either personal or related to family life. Here are some reasons why many children develop anxiety about going to school:

- "I am worried about meeting the teacher's expectations, so I don't want to go to school. If I am not there, I will not fail."
- "I don't think the kids like me. If I am not there, I won't feel the pain of rejection."
- "I am not prepared because I didn't do my work. If I don't go, I will not have to be responsible."
- "I want to stay home with Mom because she's here with the baby. I don't want to lose my mom's affection, so I'd better be here to protect my place in her heart."
- "I want to stay home to be sure Mom and Dad don't get into a fight. As long as I am home, they will be nice to each other."

From time to time, most children have feelings and thoughts like these about school. When a child is desperate or very fearful, patterns may emerge that indicate the child has a real problem about attending school. Some signals are:

- Getting sick with tummy aches or headaches on a more or less consistent basis
- Shaking and displaying nervous "ticks"
- Running a low-grade temperature
- Having sweaty hands
- Doing very manipulative "tricks" to avoid going to school

Running Away from School or Home

Creative minds seek adventure. If children don't find excitement at home or at school, they run away to find it. Children want to be challenged, both by thinking and by doing. This is a different kind of running away than by a seriously troubled child.

Keeping Children in School

Children usually can overcome school phobia when parents and teachers help them face their feelings and their responsibilities. When they know that going to school is the only choice, they will find ways to adapt.

One teacher reported that a new first-grader was avoiding school by saying he was sick when his mother encouraged him to get ready. She gave in to his wishes from time to time, so he missed enough school to get behind on his work. Then, he found other ways to avoid school. He began to have "headaches." Finally, his mother said, "I think you are pretending so you don't have to go." Then, he said, "I am not going. If you make me go, I will vomit." She said, "Oh, please don't do that." But he did. She gave in again. She called to tell the teacher, and the teacher suggested that the mother help her child face the fact that he will be going to school, even if he gets sick. The next day, he threatened again. His mother said: "I know you wish you could stay at home. Today, you wish there was no school. You will be going to school. If you need to vomit, that's okay. You may do it right here, or you may go in the bathroom. Either is fine. But you are going to school."

He did not follow through with his threat, and from then on, he went to school.

Some children depend on their parents to enforce expectations. When a parent gives in, the child does not have the maturity to know what to do. Children feel safe and secure when parents stand firm with what is acceptable and what is not. Children learn to be responsible by their parents' expectations.

- Be a confident parent or teacher. Say what you mean, and mean what you say.
- Accept children as intelligent and creative when they use threats or bribes.
- Use positive and direct statements that help children know where you stand and what you expect.
- Talk with children about their feelings, and let them know you care. Listen to their views even though you cannot condone them.

Seek professional help when children persist with symptoms of school phobia. You will know that a child needs help when a consistent pattern of school avoidance takes priority over school acceptance.

CHAPTER 5

Feelings Influence Intellect

Children take action based on how they think and how they feel. Educating our children comes down to the practical application of how children think and apply their knowledge in relation to how they feel. I call this process *biolimbics*: "bio" for the physiology and anatomy of the brain and body, and "limbic" (from the Latin *limbus*, meaning "border" or "edge") for the limbic system in the midbrain, our center for emotions. From infancy through adolescence, children are whole human beings, and they carry with them their unique talents and abilities, along with their emotional baggage. Whether grade schoolers or high schoolers, when students manifest an attachment to learning, a bond between feeling and intellect will drive them to success. Feelings provide the fuel that runs the intellectual motor, and perception guides the way.

Emotions, or feelings, play a vital role in how one thinks and how that thinking is used. Students, for example, may be brilliant thinkers with memories that far exceed our expectations, but if they are feeling inadequate or "put down" in a personal way, they may not be able to focus on their schoolwork.

Two sixteen-year-old boys engaged in a verbal battle over some academic topics. After an hour or so, it was obvious that one boy lost and felt defeated. From this point on, he began to slip in his grades and in completing his homework. His feelings of defeat and inadequacy got the best of him, and he began to sink intellectually. He needed some way to save face—to protect himself from feelings that diminished his self-worth.

Children generally enjoy performing in front of their classmates. However, if a student is ridiculed or made fun of, the desire to get in front of the class soon gives way to retreat. Students will do almost anything to avoid feelings of humiliation, especially in front of their peers. The way a child feels is every bit as important to school performance as the way a child thinks.

Too Much Emotional Baggage

Children need help to carry their emotional baggage. Support comes when parents, friends, and teachers help children "sort through" the baggage and get rid of what is "garbage." They do this by talking with children about how they feel. They listen intently as children express their ideas. When children cry, not only are parents sympathetic, but they give the child an opportunity to have a cry and still be responsible for what problems they carry. When parents "take away" the child's hurt by making excuses for them or relieving them of what is their responsibility, the child becomes weaker, not stronger. Supportive parents are able to let the child carry his or her own burdens, yet give support so the load doesn't seem so heavy.

Perception can get way off track, and a child can imagine the worst. Most children, whether six or sixteen, feel a sense of responsibility—or guilt—for what's going on at home when there are serious family problems. Some children begin to fear the loss of family stability. This fear may give way to feelings of anger and desperation.

When fear and anger escalate, rational judgment diminishes. Even the most intelligent children lose their sense of judgment when they feel desperate. Without someone to confide in and to lean on, they may lose their sense of emotional balance. If they cannot get rid of some of the emotional baggage, they begin to drown in it—or feel consumed by it. Feelings of helplessness can be as disabling as if a child were physically injured. They "choke" on the bitterness between family members that is too tough to swallow.

Children who are physically or sexually abused find ways to rationalize their own behaviors and behaviors of their parents. The emotional trauma often causes a child's stability to cave in. Many children feel such a loyalty to their parents they lie to protect them—even when this means the child will be punished. Children who know their siblings are being abused may take extreme action to put an end to the abuse. Their empathy and love for siblings, combined with fear and desperation, can lead to confusion. When children experience a loss of control, they often act out their feelings in ways that are harmful to themselves or others. They may physically injure themselves or others when they are attempting, psychologically, to eliminate the source of their fears and feelings of anger or desperation. Violent acts, such as suicide or homicide, reflect a child's loss of rational thinking, without regard for consequences.

Stability is based on experience. Children gain inner strength and a sense of hope when they know they can count on their parents and others close to them for support and love. Emotional stability—the ability to ride out the storms of stress and trauma—develops out of a child's experiencing the consistent presence of and nurturing support from at least one parent. A sense of trust and mutuality, or sharing of life with the nurturing parent, builds hope and strength within the child. When the child knows there is a parent to lean on in difficult times, attachment grows stronger.

Doesn't it seem paradoxical that a child's *inner* strength and hope come from *outside* sources? The child who experiences the consistent emotional support from others has a "lifeline" to hold on to that brings feelings of safety regardless of what happens. But when that lifeline is broken and retied with lots of breaks and frays, it may not hold when the storms of doubt and fear come crashing through with overpowering force.

Cries for Help

If children are so smart, why don't they simply tell someone they need help? Children are not only smart, but they are ingenious at detouring in order to avoid "head-on collisions." They find clever ways to dodge confrontations that might have ill effects on themselves or others. But they always send out signals when all is not well.

Many children cry out for help every day. They are sending a message: "How far do I have to go before someone will help me? I am losing control, and I need help."

As adults, we must learn to interpret their messages and respond in ways they can understand and accept.

EM Syndrome

Does your child have EM Syndrome? I call this a behavioral *escape mechanism* used by smart students to "hide" in a favorite activity in order to get out of work they are attempting to avoid. A favorite escape is to the computer or other electronic mechanism. Some students even become "addicted" to EM, with manifestations of predictable, yet difficult-to-cure, behaviors, such as getting "hooked" on electronic games or information gathering. Others may volunteer to run errands, help others, or pursue a host of non-academic tasks. EM occurs at home and at school when children and adolescents attempt to avoid academic work or certain routine chores. EM is natural but may persist and become addictive if allowed to go untreated. The best cure seems to be a dose of accountability mixed with facing the consequences, and administered with kind, yet firm, confrontation.

Freedom

Limbs shake as an old man struggling to walk against a brisk wind.
Swaying, creaking, yet not breaking.
To walk throughout the forest.
Leaves crumbling under my feet as I walk transfixed to the area as
      a whole.
Freedom to walk.
No buildings, cars, people; only trees, quiet animals, and myself.
Windows creak and pop against the wind's push.
Reminds me of home.
Never again resident.
Clouds soft and comforting as a blanket made by your grandmother.
Warm and thick enough to keep out any cold.

Yet, the clouds are cold, keeping out and extinguishing warmth.
Still, though, they are comforting.
Is that possible?
Yes.
Snow, please snow, just a flake delivered into my view.
For it is hope.
Hope of a child, innocent and not confused.
Oblivious to things around.
Only where things should be.
Optimism.
A world of optimism can fit into a small snowflake.
Let them continue.
I wish to join.

Just a note: Written as I was looking out of a classroom window. It was gray and cold outside. The wind was blowing very stiffly. It snowed later that day.

—Stephen

Fears

Four fears are commonly experienced by children and adults. These fears can stifle one's ability to think clearly and behave appropriately.

- **Fear of failure.** No one wants to fail. A student who continues to fail will find a way to succeed—even if it means succeeding as the "best failure in the class."

  A ninth-grade girl quit going to math class after failing two tests, saying there was no use in going anymore. When asked if she understood the work in class, she said she did. She experienced test anxiety because she was so fearful of failing the test. These feelings got in the way of her ability to think through and solve the math problems.

- **Fear of rejection.** Students are very sensitive to how their teachers and peers view them. When they fail to meet school expectations, they feel less than adequate. These feelings are intensified when a teacher or parent makes such statements as, "You just need to work harder, or study longer." Feelings of rejection set in when the student perceives that others can't count on her to perform with success. These feelings may be so strong that the student begins to withdraw from others.

- **Fear of humiliation.** No one likes to feel humiliated, to be put down in front of others. Students experience thoughts like, *I'd rather be dead than go through this.* Less serious feelings of humiliation are reflected by eight- to ten-year-old boys who enjoy the affection of their mothers—until their peers are present. Then, they take a more detached position, as if to say, "Mom, don't be kissing or hugging me in front of my friends—how embarrassing!" Some students feel humiliated if they can't wear the "right" clothes or shoes. And most children—young and older—detest being told they are "fat" or "dumb."

- **Fear of the unknown.** Test anxiety and feelings of panic or frustration often plague students who don't know what to expect. This is especially true on a first test in a given class. Some students accept this as a trial-and-error experience, while others take it as an all-or-none experience. Their performance may be inadequate not because they lack the know-how, but because feelings of fear overwhelm them.

By now, you may be thinking, *If they are smarter than we think, why can't they overcome these fears?* The reasons are many. In fact, they are often smart enough to protect themselves by avoiding uncomfortable situations. Many students stay home on the day of a test because they feel ill. They make themselves ill by feeling "sick" over the idea of having to take the test. Some students get together and actually talk teachers out of giving tests. Others get sick during the test and have to leave.

Children are smart, and therefore, we can help them overcome many of their fears by responding to them calmly and frankly.

Handling Fears

Step 1: Acknowledge their feelings. "It seems to me that you are really uptight about having to take your history test. You'd rather be sick than have to face that test. If I were you, I'd probably feel the same way."

Step 2: State the choices and possible consequences. "You can pull yourself together, and go to school and take the test. All I expect is that you do your best. If you fail the test, you can talk with your teacher, get help, and work at raising your average. Your teacher will know you make an effort, even though you were not feeling well.

"If you choose to stay home, there will be no radio, TV, or electronic games, and no going out. You'll need to stay in your room and in bed to rest and recover. In fact, you will not be able to go out with your friends or participate in after-school activities the rest of the week. You'll have to stay home to recover so you can do your studies."

If the student is old enough to drive, this is the time to take the keys and withhold driving privileges. If you work, this is the time to hire a "sitter" to stay with the child, regardless of the child's age, to be sure the child gets proper rest and "chicken soup." Most students will choose to go to school if they are not really sick when they know these consequences are real and will have to be faced. If they are sick, these are proper consequences.

Step 3: Give encouragement without argument. Let your child know you care and that you have confidence that things will get better. For example, say: "I know you're feeling rough. You're in no mood for tests. I'm sure that you'll do your best when you feel better. Is there anything I can do to help?"

This kind of encouragement reflects feelings of concern and respect. The child can "save face" without feeling put down. If your child attempts to "con" you, this is the time to take your parent role seriously and hold your ground.

Because children are so smart, they often test their parents to see how real the rules are and to push until they can break them. When they know that you mean what you say, many problems will be eliminated. The smarter the child, the more likely the attempt will be to start an argument. The child who is too sick to go to school is too sick to engage in an argument—this is a time to be still and quiet.

Overcoming Fears

Fears tend to build as children get older and have more experiences in living. Some very young children are not afraid of snakes and other dangerous creatures. As they learn about possibilities, and as their vision of the world broadens, they develop fears. Gradually, they learn to overcome fears when they can think through the possibilities in a reasonable way. Fears that persist are usually those brought on by strong feelings.

School phobia is a fear that many children develop as a result of fear about disappointing their parents. Test anxiety may be a fear about disappointing parents, teachers, and themselves. Performance phobia is anxiety about failing to meet expectations of others or oneself.

Balancing Stress and Risk

Believe it or not, adolescents are quite good at making judgments about behaviors that involve risk. When they take chances, they are generally aware of what they are doing. If this is so, then why do they make so many mistakes—flunking tests, having automobile wrecks, breaking legs, getting pregnant, and getting caught violating the law? Again, the reasons relate to feelings.

Fear and Worry

Mistakes usually result when stress is out of balance with risk. The smartest teens make some of the biggest mistakes because they are caught off guard. Stress, brought on by worry or fear, can throw even the most intelligent people into danger.

Many young people have personal needs, and they want satisfaction *now*. This inability to wait or to defer is often a reflection of feeling inadequate or desperate. For example, a girl who gets pregnant may be worried about losing a boyfriend, or fearful of being thought of as unacceptable. Getting sexually involved is often a result of one or both individuals needing immediate emotional fulfillment. In contrast, the person who feels adequate and secure is not easily caught in situations that compromise decision-making power. The key to avoiding accidents and making poor judgments is to develop the ability to handle stress in healthy ways.

Meeting Personal Needs

Appropriate satisfaction of personal needs brings balance into one's life. Every person seeks satisfaction of four personal needs:

1. **Physical well-being** (food, shelter, clothing, and health)
2. **Personal acceptance and a feeling of importance** (a sense of belonging, making a contribution, and dignity)
3. **A knowing that someone truly cares** (love, affection, and interaction)
4. **Protection** (knowing that someone is there for safety)

When any one of these needs goes without satisfaction from home or school, young people look elsewhere for fulfillment. When a child feels rejected by the family, anxiety and worry begin to take over. At this point, even teens who are capable of school success may begin to falter. Their emotional stability depends on meeting these personal needs. When these needs are threatened, in reality or misperception, some teens leave home and "go on the streets."

A child's early experiences within the family generally account for how that child views the outside world. Children who grow up in families they can count on for meeting physical and emotional needs usually view the world as a good place to be, a friendly world. Unfortunately, many children develop feelings of inadequacy when these needs go unmet, and they begin to view the world as unfriendly or even hostile.

Test Anxiety

Why do students suffer from test anxiety? If children are so smart, why do they panic before a test? I asked a group of high school seniors to list the reasons for having test anxiety. These topped their list:

- Wanting to please the teachers
- Wanting to meet parental expectations
- Peer expectations
- Not being adequately prepared
- A fear of failure
- A fear of losing face
- A lack of self-confidence
- Too many other things to think about
- Personal problems

Give Permission to Experience Feelings

We can help children overcome their fears by giving them permission to experience their feelings. For example, say: "Of course you're worried about your test. I would be, too. So, you're like lots of students who have test anxiety. It's natural. You are concerned about how you're going to do. Give yourself permission to feel the fear."

Use Imagination and Fantasy

Other approaches include using one's imagination and fantasy. Try this: "Before you go in to take a test, get a drink of water, and imagine that as you swallow, the water clears out all the worry and fear."

Or, "Imagine your worries going from your head down the left side of your body into your foot and out through your toes into your left shoe. Take the shoe off during the test."

Or, "Do a little dance before the test, and wiggle out all the worry."

Or, "Stand tall, put your hands on your hips, and march in place. This balances your brain and gives you extra power to carry on. If you don't want anyone to see you, go in a private place, and shut the door."

Talk about Feelings

Some students can eliminate a lot of fear and anxiety by talking about it. However, if your child is a teenager, you may not be the chosen confidant. Children at this stage often seek out peers or other adults to talk with about their fears, especially when they may be related to feelings about their parents.

In fact, "peer counseling" has a lot going for it because it's a way for teens to talk to each other without attempting to do therapy or counseling per se. They are able to release a lot of their feelings by talking. Some students have mentors to talk with about confidential thoughts and feelings.

Dramatize Feelings

Various forms of dance, music, and art provide ways for students to let go of their bothersome feelings. When they have these outlets, they tend to be more relaxed. Then, fears are not so likely to build up or be pushed back inside and hidden. Pent-up feelings have to find a release sooner or later—whether through appropriate or inappropriate behaviors. Many children who get in trouble with the law are those with pent-up feelings that have to be released. Car accidents, fights, assaults, and continuing mischief or verbal battles are often signs of letting go of feelings that have built up over time. Some may get sick as a way of releasing fears or anxieties. They may vomit or experience diarrhea or cold symptoms, all of which are physical ways of expelling "sick feelings." Of course, this does not necessarily mean that children who are sick have feelings of fear, worry, or anxiety.

> Night is a blanket of blackness covering the earth.
> Night brings fears and joys, and then they're washed away by the
> sunrise, only to be brought back by sunset.
> Night brings a sudden fear, a sudden chill, but as well a comfort, a
> warmthness.
> Something you can admire, and be afraid of.
> Something you could love and hate.
>
> —Katie Kerr

Family Life

Children who have parents available to them when they come home from school are fortunate, especially when these parents show their interest by immediate response to their school activities, class work, and other related issues. When parents show excitement about what their children accomplish, they are likely to be motivated to continue.

On the other hand, there are many children who come home to an empty, impersonal atmosphere. Their hearts sink, and the excitement they feel changes to sadness because there's no one with whom to share their day's experiences. So these children resort to filling in the sense of emptiness by numbing themselves with computer games or online preoccupations. Some go down the street to escape the emptiness by playing with other children. Some resort to street life. Self-worth diminishes when a child has little or no feedback and encouragement from the family.

Children of Divorce

Children caught up in divorce and separation may feel a loss of support from the parent outside the home, even when that parent cares deeply for the child. Other children are fortunate to have parents who make special efforts to spend time and show interest in their children even in the midst of divorce and family problems. When divorcing parents exhibit anger and stress over legal and personal differences, children pick up on the anxiety and often feel guilty. They may believe they are responsible for causing the breakup, or at least for not being able to get their parents back together again.

Children are generally more eager to talk about divorce than their parents are. In fact, many parents find ways to avoid talking about divorce because they try to protect children from the hurt and pain they, themselves, are experiencing. The sooner they and their children can deal with the reality of the situation, the better.

Many children are confused about a divorce because they cannot see the logic of it for them. They have feelings and worries that parents may not be aware of. Some of the most common include:

- A feeling of being abandoned by the parent who is outside the household.
- A sense of guilt brought about by thinking that he or she caused the parent to leave.
- Anger toward the parent who left, or toward both parents, for disrupting the family stability.
- Confusion about the disruption, especially when the child thinks the resolution is simply to be together again.

Parents who recognize these behaviors as part of the dynamics of the divorce will be able to help their children adapt to the new situation with less trauma. The following suggestions will be useful when dealing with divorce.

- **Keep the door open for communications.** Let children know it is okay to come to you and ask questions or tell you how they feel. For example, say: "I see you are worried. Is it because your daddy is not living here now? It's okay to tell me how you feel." Then give the child assurance that you will not be leaving. "You can be sure I will be here with you. Your daddy still loves you even though he will not be living here in this house."

- **Encourage the child to feel free of guilt.** "It is not your fault that Daddy left. You did not cause him to go. Your daddy and I decided we cannot live together, but we will still love you. Your daddy loves you, and I love you."

- **Make way for the child to express anger or negative feelings.** Acknowledge the child's feelings, and give permission to express these feelings in healthy ways. "You must be very angry. I see you are hitting at your friends and at me. Is it because your daddy is gone? You may feel very angry when you miss him. He left, and you cannot understand why. I know you wish he could still be here. When you feel angry, come and tell me. I will help you feel better."

- **Make way for children to respect limits.** They need guidance, especially when feelings are strong and they are feeling fragile. Here is an example to help a preschooler deal with feelings of anger: "I cannot let you hurt your friends. You can learn to be kind and gentle with your friends and your toys. But you can still have your angry feelings. You can even yell or cry or scream when you get angry, but you need to be outdoors or in your room so you won't bother others. This will help to let your feelings out. Maybe you would like to talk with Raggedy Andy (a stuffed doll) and tell him why you feel so angry. It's a good way to talk about things that make you feel bad. Or, you can use your colors and draw a picture or write a story about how you feel. Can I help you?"

  Then, start a simple conversation about the fact that Daddy is gone. For example, say: "I know you must be angry because your daddy went away. That would make me feel angry, too. But your mother is still here, and she will always be with you. Your daddy loves you, and he will come to see you, and you can go and spend the weekend with him. It won't be easy, but you will find ways to have a good time with your daddy and your mother even though they will not be together."

  Or, you might have the doll say, "Tell me why you are so angry." (Pause and wait for the child to respond.) If nothing is said, then say, "Is it because your daddy went to live someplace else and you wish he would come home?"

These kinds of openings help children think about their own feelings and begin to express them. But also give the child permission not to talk. "Maybe you don't want to talk about how you feel. That's okay. If you decide later that you have some questions or want to tell me how you feel, I will be here for you."

A child who is too young to express feelings in words still needs an opportunity to deal with anger. You may have to express the child's possible feelings and be patient. The child will find ways to work through the anger and frustration if you provide a pathway.

- **Help the child clarify confusion.** Children do not usually see or understand the reason for a divorce or separation. They think it is easy to solve by simply getting together again. One three-year-old told his mom that if his dad would come home and just watch TV and sleep with her at night, then they wouldn't have to get a divorce. That's how simple the solution is in the child's mind. The parent has to help clarify the confusion, and it may take lots of time and patience.

A mother and father came to me wanting to know why their fourteen-month-old daughter seemed to carry so much anger when things didn't go her way. Discovering that the parents were having marriage problems and doing a lot of verbal fighting with expressions of anger through their own behavior, it was easy to see how the child was absorbing these feelings. She had two models that taught her patterns of expressing her feelings. Part of her anger was likely a way to shed the feelings she had picked up from her parents. It was becoming a way of life for her. What she experienced was often repeated in her own behavior.

If the family dynamics continue to be unsettled, with lots of anger and aggressive behavior, this child likely will have problems in school. This does not mean she will develop a learning problem, but it does mean there is a good chance that she will develop a *problem about learning*. Why? Because she will be preoccupied with a sense of responsibility and guilt. *Why can't I make my parents happy? What's wrong with me?* These kinds of feelings get in the way of concentrating on schoolwork. Her emotions will put pressure on her thinking capacity, and her body and behaviors will reflect the discord.

An eighteen-month-old child has been hitting his friends at the child-care center. He is a bright and talented child, but he appears to be overly active, or "hyperactive." He flits from one activity to another, "bouncing off the walls" with anxiety. When the teachers discovered that his mother was a single parent, holding two jobs, with little time for her son, it was clear to see where much of his anxiety was seated—in his own mother. He was absorbing her frustrations as she frenetically tried to get everything done, rushing here and there with little time to relax. There simply was not much time to play together, and she felt guilty about that. Such frustrations tended to build up in the child, and he had to play them out. He will continue this pattern until his mother finds a way to settle down. Then, he will settle down, too.

Rituals

The "old brain," believed to have been the first to develop in the human, seeks rituals, traditions, and routines. The child, regardless of age, derives satisfaction and a feeling of safety by engaging in ritualistic activity.

Rituals help a person feel secure because they provide a sense of belonging. This is especially true in organizations such as schools, churches, synagogues, and temples. But rituals in the family also provide psychological connections for family members. The need to feel important is satisfied when children participate time after time in a routine fashion.

Rituals are fun and satisfying for very young children because they enjoy repetition. You may see them doing something over and over. Examples are preschoolers singing the same song many times in succession or wanting the same story read to them several times or watching the same video. Even teenagers follow much the same routine when they get home from school—snacking, listening to music, or texting friends.

Many people are so busy they forego the rituals in their lives. Routines are not as consistent as they once were. Children who are deprived of these traditional activities lack a sense of anticipation and satisfaction that comes from special events. Examples are birthday parties, family gatherings during certain holidays, reunions, evening meals, and special celebrations.

Children who have little or no ritual within the family or school often will go elsewhere to find satisfaction. Gangs commonly attract youths who have a need to belong and to feel accepted and important. Cults have their holding power in the rituals practiced by their members.

Blended Families

Adopted children and stepchildren have many adaptations to make during their childhood years. They must learn to accept one or more new parents, new places to live and play, and, often, new siblings. There may be additional grandparents and other relatives who become a part of the child's new family.

Children in some blended families sense a feeling of support from both their own parents and their stepparents. Others feel a lack of support from stepparents, especially when there are stepsiblings.

Self-Perceptions

One of the greatest challenges for adopted and foster children is acceptance of themselves because they often feel "displaced," "given away," "stolen," or "taken away." They rarely understand why their original parents are not available for them.

Since children are very centered on *the self* as they develop; they often assume they have done something bad or wrong, and therefore their parents don't want them. Such feelings can linger in a child's mind for years. Even though explanations have been given and children are in excellent care with loving adoptive or foster parents, these children tend to blame themselves. They may carry inaccurate memories that distort their thoughts and their feelings.

Many children are well-behaved when they initially enter an adoptive or foster home. They are smart enough to protect their well-being by avoiding the risk of being "put out" again. However, after they become comfortable and begin to trust their new parents, they may begin to show some of their feelings. Their behavior may take turns away from toeing the line to acting out anger and frustrations that have been building for months or years. While these expressions are not reflections on the new family, they do cause great concern and often frustration for the parents. Again, the best way to approach these children is to communicate with them, keep the door open for talking about their concerns and feelings.

Adopted and Stepchildren Seek Acceptance

These children use their social skills and their ingenuity to create a place for themselves in both the home and the hearts of their new family. They often work hard in school to gain acceptance from their parents. Adoptive children often seek ways to establish "roots" in their new setting. When they feel successful, these roots take hold with ease. But children who are unsure of their new identity and their acceptance in the adoptive or blended family may have phases of emotional instability. During these times, they may feel fragile, easily distressed, and even depressed.

The time likely will occur when an adopted child begins to ask about birth parents. This is a natural curiosity and is not a reflection on the adoptive parents. Answering a child's questions honestly and simply is usually the best approach. Give only information the child asks for to let the child know you are willing to help without adding a burden of more than the child is ready to handle. Keep the door open for communicating, and the child will come back to ask for more information when the time is right.

Both adopted and stepchildren are usually sensitive to their "new" parents, wanting to please them. Some children withhold their deeper feelings in order to shield themselves from appearing to be troublesome. They want to protect their place in the family.

Adopted and stepchildren want to be natural family members. They want to share in family rituals, fun, and responsibilities. With parents who are loving and patient, these children gradually feel a sense of belonging.

Foster Children

Foster children are always in the process of seeking a place for themselves. This seeking is not limited to a temporary family setting or shelter. The foster child is seeking to *belong,* to *be accepted,* and to *be loved* within a family that will consistently be there for life.

Many foster children are very intelligent. They know they are displaced. They feel an emptiness that cannot be filled by temporary living arrangements. They need a sense of permanence. Foster children often have problems in school because they are preoccupied with such thoughts as,

Who am I? Where do I belong? Who cares about me? and *I must not be worthy enough to have my own family.*

Foster parents are faced with the task of caring for a foster child without making an attachment that has deep emotional ties. This is difficult, especially with young children. Parents who work toward adoption with a foster child are helping solve the problem of a child living in limbo.

Foster children need lots of support from the parents and family members, school personnel, professionals, and friends. They are pursuing life with a handicap of the absence of consistent love and emotional stability from the same family.

Many foster children, however, succeed in school and in life. These children tend to have a strong sense of self, hope from within, and a motivation to experience success. But they must have help along the way.

Grandparenting

If you're a grandparent, then you have something special to offer to children that no one else can give. Why are "grands" so great?

They are emotionally as well as physically tied to their grandchildren, yet a generation removed. This position embodies them with a sense of awe from the child's view. Awe, from the root meaning "authority," surrounds you, and children view you as omnipotent, full of wisdom and power.

Grandparents represent an image of love and warmth. Children enjoy being close, hugging, and making lots of contact.

Grands are comfortable with themselves, and this makes children comfortable, too. You can laugh and play, tell stories, philosophize, or just be there, and the children are content.

A friend of mine who's a grandfather of four said, "Being a grandparent is a desirable diversion from the daily routine. It's a legitimate way to have fun and enjoy the ridiculous."

Many grands play the role of mentor for their grandchildren. A mentor is a teacher, confidant, and role model. They often have a powerful influence on young minds because children seem to sense their wisdom. Because they are two generations removed, they pose no threat, as aspiring parents often do. Children do not feel the same "bump up against" them. They are open to what grandparents share—and suggest.

There's another side, too. That's the frustration and difficulty grandparents often feel in their reluctance to impose limits when parents allow their children to "get by" with misbehaviors. As one grandmother put it, "Reflecting on the child-rearing years often gets me into trouble with my daughter. I want to make recommendations, but she takes it as criticism."

Sometimes children take advantage of conflicts between parents and grandparents, and push the limits. They learn to pit one adult against the other. Children are especially sensitive to differences in feelings between parents and grandparents.

Try these helpful hints when dealing with grandchildren:

1. **Acknowledge your own adult children** for their parenting skills so they don't feel like you're criticizing them. For example, say, "You have your hands full with the baby and the three-year-old. It's not easy keeping up with them and your job. I don't know how you do it." This helps a parent feel the comfort of your empathy, and the likelihood of her listening to you is greater.

2. **Limit your advice.** Sometimes it's better to grin and bear it than to interfere. Part of the pain of being a parent is to cross hurdles that seem impossible. Without the pain and consequences, parental responsibility may give way to apathy, frustration, neglect, or even abuse.

3. **Qualify your advice.** "You're Johnny's mother, and you have to live with what you do. I have the advantage of saying good-bye when things get rough. So you may want to pitch my free advice—it's shared with love and concern." Then say it. Then stop.

4. **Discuss differences about limits in private with the parents.** Negotiate the terms, and then hold to them. For example, when at the child's home, follow the family rules; when at the grandparents', follow their rules. Grandparents can then feel free to intervene when the child gets out of hand.

Grandparents Raising Children

Many grandparents take on the role of parents for their grandchildren. Some have legal custody or guardianship, and others adopt. This is an awesome task requiring grandparents to shift gears during the later years to provide parenting again. These grandparents need support from relatives and friends as they dedicate time, energy, and money to bringing up another generation. They may need professional help to work through difficulties with the children's parents.

Grandfather Crawford

Grandfather Crawford is a very nice man. His full name is Norman Theodore Crawford Jr. He was born in Flint, Michigan, in the year 1936. He is still alive. His is my father's father, and now lives by a lake in Kingston, Oklahoma. Now he is retired, but before he was in the Marines and the Korean War in the years of 1954 to 1959. Grandfather Crawford met Grandma while stationed in Japan in the year of 1955. Grandfather Crawford knows sign language because his father was deaf.

Talking to him and working on the computer are my favorite activities to do with him. He is a very, very special grandfather to me. He takes me fishing sometimes, and I like to ride in the boat with him and my family. He was a high school football star player and was in the newspaper. At the lake, many dogs like him and visit his house. He has a green thumb because he grows great vegetables. He grows tomatoes, potatoes, pumpkins, green peppers, onions, beans, cucumbers, carrots, and all kinds of vegetables and some fruit, too. Grandmother makes pickles out of the cucumbers, and they are really good. He is a very smart man like my father, and signs really fast. He likes to take us on the tractor and to drive along to the lake and to watch other boats.

He taught me how to work on the computer, and teaches me some different old sign language. He wanted me to be a very smart and creative girl, and also taught me some different things. He wanted to grow good vegetables so Grandmother could cook them. He loves to work on the computer and works on it exactly every day, and sometimes studies. When I work on the games or projects that he taught me on the computer, it reminds me of him. He was so special to me, and I also have good memories of him.

—Courtney L. Crawford

Dealing with Death

Holidays and birthdays often magnify the sadness for families who have faced the death of a child or family member. Friends may feel inadequate in expressing their sympathy on special days and, therefore, avoid the grieving of parents and family members.

When a Child Dies

Parents don't really get over the death of a child. They have to find ways to deal with it, acknowledge it, and remember the good times they shared.

Sometimes it takes months before parents can bring themselves to go into a child's room to clear out personal belongings. The emptiness ushers in feelings of loss and a sense of despair. These feelings are natural, yet parents must find ways to carry on fulfilling lives with their current family.

It's important for families to give themselves permission to feel sad, even though it may have been several years since a child's death occurred. Looking at pictures and reminiscing over special family moments helps to mend the wounds of empty feelings. But it's not always easy to bring those memories to the surface.

I had a mother tell me she lost two daughters at the same time. One was eighteen and the other was sixteen years old. The sisters needed to go to the store to pick up some things for the senior prom. Her other child, a thirteen-year-old son, was denied permission by the sisters to go with them, as is often the case with teenage siblings. The girls were killed in a car accident on the way home. The mother, a divorced single parent, closed the door to the daughters' bedroom and had not entered for more than a year.

She approached me after a workshop and told me her son was angry and aggressive in his behavior both at home and at school. She was beside herself in knowing what was wrong and what to do. I suggested that she do physically what she also needed to do psychologically—go into the girls' room, and sort out their things and let go of them. I also suggested that her son help her in this process.

It is natural for the remaining children to go through behavioral changes after the death of a sibling. They often misbehave because they are feeling guilty, angry, or rejected, and this is a way to be punished. Even though such behavior doesn't solve the problem, it is often a child's way of dealing with unresolved feelings. In this case, the brother felt guilty that he lived while his sisters died. It was also difficult for the thirteen-year-old because he didn't have the chance to reconcile his anger with his sisters for not letting him go along with them to the store.

Feelings and Thoughts about Losing a Loved One

There are several phases that one goes through when faced with the death of a loved one—denial, anger, grief, and resolution. These phases may take weeks or months to be experienced.

When a person is stuck in anger, like this boy was, he has to deal with those feelings before making it to the resolution.

Going through his sisters' things and being able to talk about them was the start of dealing with the reality he faced. His mother later told me that he cried, cursed, and shouted. Finally, he settled into talking with his mom about his feelings. His thoughts were shared, too. For a while before the "clearing out" process, he considered suicide as a way to "even the score."

It's an awesome task for a parent to talk to children about their deceased sibling, but it is a vital part of the healing process. When a person never wants to talk about this, it may be a signal that professional help is needed. Counselors, psychologists, social workers, psychiatrists, clergy, and family physicians provide such services. There are times when a teenager will talk with a family friend, or even a peer, about the pain and feelings of loss.

Acknowledging the Loss

Facing the loss of a loved one is a unique experience for each person. We each have our own set of feelings and perceptions, and how we deal with these has to fit within our personal framework. It is the element of loss that we share in common.

Sharing in memorial or funeral services is a way of acknowledging the death of someone we love while giving one another emotional support. I think it's important for even very young children to attend the memorial or funeral service. Although they may not understand it, they will know that something special and different is happening, and this gives them permission to feel different, too. Later, they will remember the occasion and be able to talk about it and ask questions that will help them to understand. Some children who are not allowed to participate in the ceremonials grow up with resentment and blame their parents for depriving them of participating.

Friends can help ease the pain of holidays for bereaved parents simply by acknowledging that it is a difficult time for them. Many times people avoid visiting on such holidays as birthdays and Memorial Day because they don't know what to say or do. But this is when a family or a parent needs support. Just dropping by with a bouquet to let her know you care is enough. If she wants to talk, you'll know it.

The most important thing on such a visit is to have an awareness of the person's feelings and respond in a gentle, caring way. You'll know intuitively if the person wants to talk. Sometimes it is just as well to be quiet and kind. This is a time to *avoid* such statements as, "I know how you must feel," "This was meant to be," or, "It's going to be all right."

More appropriate are such statements as, "I cannot imagine how you must feel," "I am here to express my love and concern," and, "Let me know how I can help."

Holidays Bring Forth Memories

Holidays are often difficult times for families who have lost a child. This can be especially hard on single parents, since they have no one with whom to share their deepest grief, particularly when they have faced the death of an only child. Therefore, a sudden change in a person's behavior is natural during the stress of holidays. A person might even be curt or resentful of being around someone who has children.

The key is to be sensitive to these people. Simply saying "I know this is a hard day for you, and I'm here if you need me" is often enough. Perhaps the best advice is to be caring, sensitive, and available, and let the parent know, "I really miss her, too."

Community Life

Some children are fortunate to live in neighborhoods where there is a sense of community. The "granny" next door is always interested in what the children have to say. The man down the block talks with his teenage friends about their ideas on politics. Several families get together for picnics and outings. Children play outdoors with one another, running, climbing trees, and building dreams.

Other children live in residential settings in which no one knows who his neighbor is. There is little interest in what goes on with children outside their own "walls."

Some children go to schools in which the teachers know every child in their classrooms and many of the other children as well. They show genuine interest in each child's abilities and progress in school. Other children attend schools in which there are too many children in each class for a teacher to know them personally. A teacher has to look at a seating chart to call a student by name.

School is the one place that every child looks to with expectations of support and safety. Teachers and school personnel may be the most significant people in the lives of some children, especially those who are estranged from their own families.

Mentoring

Mentor refers to a person who serves as a teacher or role model of the highest order. The mentor makes a commitment to share time with a student in order to guide that student through a meaningful learning experience. The mentor often serves as a role model in a given area of expertise, or as a person of influence. Examples are mathematicians who serve as mentors for students to pursue math as a career, or an artist who takes on a student as an apprentice.

A young child may be drawn to an older person, who becomes an informal teacher or mentor. This is often a person who takes a special interest in the child and sees his or her potential.

Mentor Relationships

Mentors provide a powerful source of support for children because they develop meaningful relationships as they interact. High school and college students who are fortunate to have mentors often excel and reach both short-term and long-term goals. The student feels empowered by the confidence the mentor communicates. The student feels that "someone really believes in me."

If every school child had a mentor relationship with one teacher, education would be a success. The interpersonal connection between the mentor and student provides a powerful emotional tie that gives enormous energy for pursuing academic tasks. Such a relationship, while not focused on emotional and personal problems, often serves as a *psychological bridge* for the child to cross "psychological barriers" that might otherwise prevent success in school and in life. The mentor is able to help the student see more options, more possibilities, and more progress.

If every child "on the street" had a mentor relationship with one upstanding adult citizen, life would look brighter for everyone. Children need to see themselves in the "mirrors" reflected by their mentors.

We often hear that the "era of the hero" is over. Perhaps that is so, and perhaps that absence will make way for entrance of the "era of the mentor." A hero is someone perceived as worthy of being emulated. Heroes are idolized individuals with whom a child rarely has direct personal contact. Children have vicarious idealizations about themselves becoming like their heroes. Examples are TV and movie stars, sports figures, musicians, and historical figures. However, these notions often fade when new idols or heroes enter center stage, and children shift to a new fantasy of themselves in relation to the new heroes. This, of course, does not negate the fact that many children have grown up to be highly successful and self-confident individuals as the result of having hero idols. Yet, consider the greater value for children in having *personal contact* with recognized individuals who take genuine interest in them.

Children often respond positively to mentors because they are once removed from parents. There is not the threat of being "so close to the call." As children approach adolescence, they naturally shy away from the parent and even become defiant. This is their way of breaking out and establishing their own identity. This is a time when they especially need an adult confidant, one who recognizes and accepts them without "personal strings" attached.

Leadership

Teachers who are leaders generally make progress because they inspire students to want to do their work. In contrast, teachers who are managers often push children to get their work done. No one likes to be pushed—and students often resist.

Leaders look for the talents and capabilities of each student and then engage the student in taking action on his or her own behalf.

Leaders look for the talents and capabilities of each student and then engage the student in taking action on his or her own behalf.

CHAPTER 6

Behavior

I s your child's behavior a continuing concern? This may be a sign that your child is smarter than you think. Misbehavior, or what we perceive as misbehavior, is often a reflection of the child's ability to adapt to circumstances—or to send out a call for help. Whether age two, twelve, or sixteen years old, children have a way of knowing how to engage a parent— usually to get what they need or want!

A couple came to me with concerns about their seven-year-old son, Cal. Their main concern was his behavior at home. In school, he was doing excellent work, the teacher liked him, and he liked school. But at home, it was a different story. While the parents treated him like the other two children—one age four, and the other, nine—Cal seemed to be causing upheaval at every turn—fighting with his sister, refusing to play with his older brother, ignoring parent requests, and continually asking his mother for affection. Cal was sending a powerful message: "I need attention. I need attention. I feel caught between my little sister and older brother. Nobody likes me; I can't do anything right. Why should I try?

I'll never be as smart as my brother, and I'll never get the attention my sister gets."

These messages were not spoken directly, but instead were both subtle and expressed through actions rather than words. Cal is very bright and smart enough to get attention from his parents—even for the wrong reasons. Let's take a look at what he's able to do.

First, Cal is using misbehavior to get attention. Second, he is careful not to say something that will offend his mother, and third, he uses affection rather than destruction when engaging his mother. She said he continually comes to her, saying, "Mom, can I have a hug? I love you. Please hold me. Do you love me?" She said he does this so much that sometimes she has to walk out and go to the neighbors to get relief. She said, "He's like a leech, hanging on for dear life."

But this behavior is powerful and caries several unspoken messages that reflect his own insight. Here are a few of Cal's underlying thoughts:

- I want to be sure that I am important to you.
- I have doubts about my self-worth.
- I need your assurance that I am acceptable.

These messages indicate that Cal feels inferior or inadequate in some way. He shows this by being a "charming nuisance." Then it backlashes when his mom can't take it any longer and walks out. Her message (not in words either) is: "I don't know what to do, and I cannot face this any longer—I must have a break."

But Cal interprets the walkout as: "I knew it. She doesn't love me. I'm not worthy of her hugs. She can't stand to have me close to her, so she leaves me. I must be awful."

What is so smart about Cal's misbehavior with his sister and brother? First, it brings him attention because the parents get involved in order to stop the fighting. Cal would rather be punished than be ignored. Second, he feels important when he wields his power—even though it brings punishment. Third, he compensates for losing control of himself by gaining control of others.

You might say, "But he isn't solving the problem." While that is true, he is smart to push the limits enough with his behavior that parents seek advice. So, Cal's call for help worked.

Most children who get into trouble are calling for help. However, they are smart enough not to put their heads on the chopping block—or at least not to let the ax fall. They use their charm and affection, or their appearance of disability, to lure the adult's attention to their own perceived inadequacy. The first thing the adult usually thinks is, *What am I doing wrong?* or, *Why can't I handle this child?* So the child is smart enough to deflect, frustrate, or confuse the adult.

Now the big question is what to do to help a child like Cal without damaging his self-esteem? If the child is so smart, why doesn't he behave appropriately in the first place? Let's look at what may be going on within the child:

- He is testing the validity of his own self-doubt by pushing his mother to the limit to see what she will do. If she stands firm, she can send such messages as:
  o "I love you because you are my child."
  o "I accept you as you are."
  o "I will help you build respect for yourself and others by helping you find ways to interact without clinging or fighting."
  o "I will help you direct your energy in positive ways."
- He has already given the indication that he is ready to take action on his own behalf—that's what he's been doing even though with unacceptable behavior.

If Cal is smart enough to cause so much turmoil, he's smart enough to take a new path toward feeling adequate and acceptable.

Guiding Behavior

Setting Limits

Limits that are built around *respect* are effective and give meaning to guidance of children's behavior. Four areas of respect form boundaries that encompass the limits that build character and help children develop patterns for responsible and caring behavior.

1. **Respect for self.** Every child needs to develop an awareness of self and respect for oneself.
2. **Respect for others.** Holding others in esteem as valued and important individuals and group members builds attitudes of respect for others.
3. **Respect for property.** As children learn to care for their own toys and for property around them, they develop a sense of ownership and concern for what is theirs and what belongs to others. They also learn respect for mutually owned property.
4. **Respect for nature.** A reverence for nature gradually becomes a part of the child's character as experiences are provided that help develop ideas about beauty and the value of plant and animal life.

These four domains of respect make it relatively simple for adults to set limits and enforce them. As long as these domains are not violated, the limits are honored. Children have an easier time accepting limits when they mean something to them personally. Too many limits become confusing and are too difficult to enforce. Each time we set a limit, we need to ask a few questions:

1. Is this limit needed to develop respect in one or more of the four domains?
2. Does the child really need this limit, or is it repetitious?
3. Will the child be able to understand this limit or the reason for it?
4. Will this limit contribute to the individual, family, or group for which it is being imposed?
5. Is there an existing limit that can be eliminated to make way for this new limit?

You can see by these questions that children need as few limits as possible. Only those necessary for their development and for the safety and good of those around them ought to be considered.

Of course, some limits are necessary, even when a child cannot understand or accept the reason for them. In such a case, the adult must establish the limit and enforce it.

Believe it or not, most school-aged children at this stage want rules and limits. When they play games with one another, they are insistent upon following the rules—and, "If you don't, you can't play!"

One father of a four-year-old reported having a very difficult time preventing his son from throwing his toys while playing in the family room. He said he was really concerned about what to do. He had started spanking him. I suggested that he talk with him, so he did. Later he reported to me that when he talked with the child about his misbehavior, the child replied, "But Dad, I'm only four years old—I haven't had time to learn yet how to behave."

As long as children follow these rules of respect, they have lots of latitude and freedom. When they break one of these rules, they must face the consequences. Take the case of eight-year-old Doug. He's old enough to talk about what the consequences might be. Usually denying a privilege—such as TV watching, bike riding, or computer games— is adequate. Give him one chance to behave respectfully. When Doug persisted in misbehavior, then the consequences were imposed.

The adult's action is equally as important as the child's. Doug has been seeking his mother's attention. She was wise to give him affection and send messages of love in a variety of ways—when he was engaged in appropriate behavior—so he wouldn't have to misbehave to get it. When he arrived at home after school, they would have a few minutes together with a snack. She commented on his schoolwork in positive ways, such as by saying, "So, you had ten math problems, and you got six of them right. That's great; you only missed four." This sends a message of respect for him and his efforts. Think of the message Doug would have gotten if she had said, "You had ten problems, and you missed four. You could work those last night, so what's wrong with your memory?" The fact is the same in either case: six problems correct, and four problems incorrect. Nothing will change that. But the next time, Doug may work to get more problems correct in order to again hear positive statements from his parents. While Doug is playing, his mother might simply walk by and say, "Doug, I sure enjoy being your mom.

I'm so glad you're a part of our family." This is a message of love, and Doug will feel it as well as hear it.

Enforcing Limits

Take action to enforce limits.

Action 1: Remain calm. The child is out of control; you are in control. Your disposition will help the child settle down sooner when you keep your composure.

Action 2: Use the child's name in positive ways. Eliminate the name when correcting misbehavior.

If you really want to change your child's behavior, *stop using the child's name when misbehavior occurs.* It really works! The task here is to connect the child's name with appropriate behavior to build a positive self-image and to encourage appropriate behavior. Children will do almost anything to have their names called. When a child hears his name, he feels important—even for the wrong behavior. A child's name is a hallmark, a trade name in the family. Doesn't it seem contradictory that we give a child a name and then use it against the child? Children respond to their names quickly. Knowing this, we can transform most of misbehavior into appropriate behavior—simply by how we use a child's name.

So what does one do when a child is across the room and is engaging in destructive behavior that requires the adult's attention? Get up, go over to the child, and *gently touch* the child on the shoulder (this anchors the contact in the child's brain); then say to the child (without using the name), "Let me help you," or, "What is it that you want?"

These are disarming statements that most children respond to with attention to the adult. Then talk with the child about the situation and what can be done. Proceed to the next action.

Action 3: Talk with the child in positive *what-to-do* statements, and avoid negative or *"don't"* statements of what not to do.

This is a time to guide the child, not to simply reprimand. The child's brain is such that under the age of about ten years, the right hemisphere helps activate *action verbs* and *what* statements faster than negative ones.

For example, when we say, "Don't hit your sister," the brain hears those words but processes, "Hit your sister." Also:

- "Don't throw the ball indoors" becomes "*Throw* the ball indoors."
- "Don't step in the mud" becomes "*Step* in the mud."
- Children respond quickly to action verbs and statements of *what to do*. Examples are:
- "Be gentle with your sister."
- "Take the ball outdoors."
- "Tell your sister what you want to do."

Children are smart and often can help to resolve their own problems. First, identify the problem: "It looks like you're having trouble sharing. Sometimes it's hard to share what belongs to you." This kind of statement helps the child clarify the problem while making a break in the action.

Then, ask the children to get involved: "What do you think you can do? You have one tricycle, and there are two of you." Wait for one child to respond. If the child says he or she doesn't know, or, "I want it!" then say something like, "I'll hold the tricycle while we talk about it. You can take turns, or you can share and play together."

Then say to one child, "You can say to your sister, 'I'm playing with it now. When I finish, you can use it.'"

Then say to the other, "You can say to your brother, 'May I use it when you finish?' or, 'Let's play with it together.'"

Usually, one child will act on his or her own words.

Action 4: Attend to the victim first, and *avoid taking sides*.

When a child is hurt, go to that child first, and give attention to be sure the child is all right. Give tender loving care. Then, turn to the aggressor, if there is one, and make a statement such as: "Let me help you. You must play with respect. Remember, that's one of our rules. Respect means you are kind and use words to talk about what you want and how you feel. Now, what can you do so you can play again?"

Follow up by giving children examples of what to say, such as, "Stop pushing me," or, "It hurts when you push me down."

If a child says, "I'm sorry," that's fine, but you will be wise not to force a child to say, "I'm sorry." Again, children are smart, and they soon learn to say the "magic words," and it's okay to misbehave again. Most children are not sorry when they strike at another child—they are expressing their real feelings, and they mean it. To make them say, "I'm sorry" is to do violence to their integrity.

Avoid taking sides, even though you may have seen what happened. Children are smart enough to work through their differences, and when adults take sides, children take advantage. They begin to "con" adults into taking "my" side in order to feel more important. Adults who step back and let children work out their own problems will see respect and the "art of negotiating." You might even say, "You can negotiate."

Then explain what the word means. They like new words --the bigger the better-- and they remember what the words mean, especially when they are directly involved.

Action 5: Be an example, and *model the kind of behavior you expect.*

Parents are *models* for their children—the best teachers children will ever have. Children are so smart they absorb both the feelings of their parents and the message that is sent by parent behavior.

Parents who fight by shouting and using word-battles will see their children learning to argue and getting into verbal wars. Parents who fight in physical ways see their children fighting in similar ways to get what they want.

Parents who talk, discuss, and argue with respect for each other see their children taking on these patterns. The calmer the parent, the calmer the child. Children often think they must live up to their parents' expectations. When they see parents fighting and cursing and complaining, they think they will be recognized for the same kinds of behaviors. After all, children see parents as the most important people in their lives, so, "What's good enough for them is good enough for me."

What You Expect Is What You Get

Parents usually get the behaviors they expect from their children. Why is this so? One reason is that children are smart. They sense what the parent expects. They build their own sense of self on the basis of parent expectations. When the parent says:

- "You are more trouble than I can handle," the child sees herself as a troublemaker.

- "How many times do I have to tell you . . .?" the child begins to think, *There is something wrong with me.*
- "How can you be so dense?" the child begins to think, *I must be dumb.*
- "When will you ever learn?" the child begins to think, *Maybe I can't learn.*

Children store these messages in the brain and use them as ways to measure success or failure—self-worth. A child who hears such put-down statements often lives out these themes in everyday behavior. A child will do almost anything to uphold his or her own image as reflected by parents or other important people.

Children who are smart enough to misbehave in order to get attention, to demonstrate their need for control, to get revenge, or to live up to expectations of failure are also smart enough to develop patterns of appropriate behavior to meet their personal needs. There are three basic needs that every child seeks to satisfy:

- To feel like someone truly cares
- To feel like physical needs are being met
- To feel important in the eyes of others

Moral Development

Children, like adults, are social by nature. They want to belong, first to the family, and then to circles of friends, school classes, and various social groups. Getting along with others includes respecting social rules and moral values. One of the most important roles of parents is to guide their children through the early years of building relationships based on trust and mutual understanding.

Three Stages of Moral Development

As children progress in growth and personality formation, they experience three stages of moral development. Parents play a different role in each of these stages as children move along the pathway to adulthood.

Stage 1: Impulsive behavior. Jean Piaget, the great Swiss psychologist, called this the stage of "motor rule." *Motor* here refers to the body telling the child what to do. From infancy to about five or six years of age, children often act on impulse. They do what they feel like in an instant, without regard for the consequences.

During these first five years, parents serve as the child's social conscience. That is, the parent has to stop certain actions to protect the child or others, or to protect property. Also, the parent has to help the child feel free and safe to act within certain limits. Otherwise, the child has no way to gain a sense of trust and respect for self and others.

These early years are filled with experiences in which children interact with their parents. When there are no rules or limits, children grow up thinking they can do anything. When there are no patterns for respecting rules or guidance, children often become chaotic or confused. Their impulses guide their actions.

Children are bright and quickly learn what they can get by with and how to detour around the rules or limits. The fact they are so smart also indicates they can learn to follow guidelines and limits. They can build patterns of self-control. These patterns are based on three factors:

- Examples set by parents
- Experiencing consequences when limits or rules are violated
- Trust in parents that someone will be there to stop the children if they venture beyond the boundaries of safety and respect

Children who, in the first five or six years, learn the meaning of respect—for self, others, property, and nature—will practice these throughout their lives. Parents who help children develop a conscience orientation are setting the stage for sound decision making later. Our world is filled with laws and rules that make way for protection of people's well-being. A sense of trust and mutual respect has its roots in the early experiences of trusting relationships with parents.

Common sense is born out of consistent patterns of facing natural and logical consequences of cause and effect. When early patterns are in place, children grow up knowing what to expect if rules are violated and what to do to solve problems.

Stage 2: Respect for authority. Piaget referred to this stage as "coercive rule," or respect for "rules of the game." Children between about six and eleven years of age go through a natural inclination to follow the rules. This is especially true when children have had consistent guidance in the first stage.

By this time, children are open to logic that is shared by others. They can play by the rules because they understand the purpose of rules. They listen to teachers and parents as authorities. They like to please adults.

There's a secret to maintaining respect from your children. As long as you keep a *balance between love/affection and awe/fear*, your child will behave with respect. Children are so smart they calculate just how many times they can get by with something before you stop them—or get angry. When they keep pushing the limits, it's a cue that you are losing your "awe," or sense of authority. To get it back, you must mean what you say—and say what you mean. Many parents give lots of love and affection but are short on consequences for misbehavior. Balance these, and you can relax.

Stage 3: Mutual respect. This is the stage of *reciprocal rule*. During adolescence, children actually reflect the results of the first stage of life. That is, their *roots of morality* are grounded in the first two or three years of life. When their sense of trust and mutuality is strong, they will make judgments about what is in the best interest of others as well as themselves. They will exercise respect for opinions and differences of others, yet be able to hold on to their own ideas. They are willing to follow social rules because they see the benefits. On the other hand, children who grow up without a sense of trust and mutual respect often resort to immature judgments and unacceptable behaviors during the adolescent years.

Even though teenagers tend to defy their parents and take opposition to their wishes, they are capable of making sound judgments. Pursuing their last big push for independence means testing the reality of their parents. Do parents really stand for what they say is important? Do they set rules for the sake of everyone's well-being, or for the sake of setting rules? Teenagers who grow up with lots of trust and sharing with parents during the first years of life ultimately will exercise these patterns with others. When they change the "rules of the game," it's with mutual consent of the players.

Common Behavioral Concerns

Typical behavioral problems will be observed in all children from time to time. Smart children tend to display problems as a way of calling attention to themselves, or to call for help. Since children are not mature, or confident enough to talk directly about their feelings and perceptions, they often act out in some form of misbehavior. Most typical problems have appropriate alternatives. Look over the following list to score a child's behavior. If a child scores higher on the left list and lower on the right, the challenge is to move that child toward the appropriate behavior. If a child's score is higher on the right, that child is forming attitudes and values that lead to appropriate behaviors.

Impulsive outbursts .... Focus

Power struggles .... Self-control

Anger .... Understanding

Bullying .... High self-esteem

Defiance .... Respect

Fighting .... Communication skills

Destructive aggression .... Responsible action

Overactivity .... Calmness and confidence

While the above behaviors represent a range of difficulties that children must learn to manage, they are part of normal development. Children generally develop social skills and adapt to changes with the help of parents and teachers who serve as good models for them. Children also learn appropriate behaviors when adults interact and communicate with respect and firm guidance.

Biting

Why do very young children engage in biting behaviors? Because they are smart. They learn quickly what gets results. Consider the child who bites another child on the wrist or forearm to get a toy. The victim drops the toy, and the biter gets it. However, because children are smart, they also can learn there are appropriate ways to play without hurting others.

Children generally go through two major stages of biting, one from about ten to twenty months, and another during the latter half of the second year. When we understand why children bite, we are enabled to help them overcome this impulsive behavior.

Reasons for Biting

1. **Affection.** Yes, children bite to show their feelings of love as well as their feelings of anger. Children who bite to show affection usually leave their mark on the face of another child—or adult—or on a front part of the body, such as the upper arm or shoulder. Children who have been receiving kisses from parents and others learn to show affection with the lips. As they approach the first stage of biting, they often express their affection for others by kissing. When teeth are in place, they use them to help express this affection. Adults often let children kiss them on the nose, cheeks, and even the mouth. When the infant gets teeth and bites on the face, it brings attention suddenly to the fact the child is no longer in early infancy.

2. **Exploration.** Children who bite to explore and learn usually leave their marks on the faces or other parts of the body that have exposed skin. Children learn through their bodies and senses, especially during the *sensory motor period* in the first two years of life. As we know, infants tend to put everything in their mouths during the first year or so. This is one of the most effective ways for them to learn about an object. By this same method, they learn what it feels like to bite into something, flesh being no exception. Biting a human feels different from biting a toy, a piece of carrot, or a teething ring. Children learn by exploring, whether with their eyes, hands and fingers, feet, or their teeth.

3. **Control.** Children who bite as a means of control usually leave their marks on another's forearm, wrist, or hand. This type of behavior usually brings quick results, such as the victim dropping whatever is in hand. The biting child learns very quickly that this is a way to get results. This kind of biting is more "contagious" than any other because children see that it works.

4. **Aggression.** Children who bite to show aggression usually leave their marks on another's back or the backside of arms or shoulders. This is a form of attack and is considered a signal that the biting

child needs help to express anxiety, frustration, or anger in a manner that is not destructive or injurious to others.

5. **Anxiety.** Some children bite themselves on their hands or gnaw on their wrists when they are worried or frustrated. This is a clue that something is wrong.

How to Handle Biting Behavior

Each form of biting requires a particular kind of response. Since children are quick to learn, parents make a big mistake when they bite back. This only teaches the child that biting is an acceptable form of behavior since their parents do it. Spanking, in most cases, is also ineffective because it teaches the child to shift from biting to hitting.

Each situation is a little different and therefore calls for careful judgment on the part of a parent or teacher. Consider the following suggestions.

1. **Always attend to the victim first.** Give plenty of TLC. Cleanse the wound thoroughly, and keep an eye on the injured area for possible changes in skin color or swelling.

2. **Avoid using the biting child's name.** Avoid giving reinforcement or attention to this behavior by connecting the child's identity with the biting behavior. Show the child what can be done by giving simple verbal instructions: "Stop. I will help you learn to be kind and gentle."

3. **Separate the child from the others for a short time** (a minute or so). One of the best ways to do this is to hold the child by the wrist, keeping the child next to you as if "in captivity." Children want to be free to play, and they learn quickly that biting prevents this freedom. Do not hold the child by the hand, as this is an affectionate gesture. Never carry the "biter" because this is also affectionate. Some children learn quickly by being placed in "time out." The message to send is, "We want you to play and have a good time, and in order to do so, you must learn to be kind to others."

4. **Take note of circumstances that may have caused the biting.** Determine which of the reasons is most likely to precipitate biting behavior. Redirect the child's behavior to help the child learn there

are appropriate ways to show affection, explore, or exercise one's will, without hurting others.

5. **Provide plenty of activities and materials that engage children in stage-appropriate play.** Examples are manipulative toys, play dough, tearing colored paper, scribbling and coloring, finger-painting, working puzzles, stacking toys, and playing with dolls and puppets.

6. **Children who bite themselves need help.** Parents and caregivers can help by talking with the child. For example, "I see that you are upset. Perhaps you are worried about something." Then talk about possible reasons. Even when a child is too young to talk, he or she gets the idea that you are concerned and want to help. This may be enough to ease the anxiety. Some children may need professional help to unravel anxieties and provide therapy and support.

Crying

Nature has endowed babies with crying ability for two main reasons:

- To communicate needs or discomfort—such as hunger, thirst, or pain.
- To bring the parent near.

Parents generally learn to recognize different cries of a baby—for hunger, pain, to be held and cuddled, to bring the parent into view, or to make physical contact.

Should babies be allowed to cry for long periods of time? No. A baby's cry should be broken with a gentle voice and close cuddling. Crying too long places the body under stress. Babies need to regain balance in their vital processes—heartbeat, blood pressure, and breathing processes.

What Parents Can Do about Crying

1. Observe and detect the probable reasons for crying, and eliminate them when possible.
2. Give plenty of TLC during times when the baby is not crying.
3. Be sure basic needs are met—nourishment, comfort, interpersonal and eye contact, stimulation, space, and freedom for exploring.

4. Interrupt a long siege of crying by lifting the baby and cuddling and talking in a gentle voice. When everything is checked— diapers clean, hunger satisfied, no particular reason for pain—put the child down. Reassure the child by such statements as, "I believe you are okay. If you still feel like crying, it's okay. I'll be here. You may watch me or play with your toys." Even though infants don't understand the words, they get the idea.

Thumb-Sucking and Pacifiers

Sucking is an inborn human characteristic. Even after the sucking reflex has subsided, children learn that sucking brings a source of satisfaction.

Reasons for Thumb-Sucking

- Sucking brings pleasure.
- When the breast or bottle is no longer available, some infants resort to thumb- or finger-sucking.
- Thumb-sucking serves as a link between the parent and child.
- The infant may be hungry or thirsty.
- Sucking the thumb may be a habit pattern formed during the prenatal period.

What about Pacifiers?

Pacifiers are usually more beneficial for parents than for children. They keep the child quiet, and parents feel less frustration. However, pacifiers are not necessary for children. They prevent children from natural development.

Pacifiers often prevent speech development. When a toddler is ready to talk, words cannot wait. A child with a pacifier in her mouth will not take it out to speak. A child without a pacifier will speak immediately when a thought is ready for expression. Even a child who is sucking his thumb will automatically withdraw the thumb as the words are spoken. But with a pacifier, the child has to deliberately remove it from the mouth—by then, the words are lost.

Pacifiers build a sense of dependency. Children who use pacifiers depend on having something in their mouths for satisfaction. They will likely be smokers, "snackers," or "chewers" as they get older.

Pacifiers may cause drooling. Some children drool saliva as they suck on pacifiers. This also can interfere with proper breathing. The mouth should be free to open and close as necessary for natural and healthy breathing without obstructions or extra saliva.

What Parents Can Do
1. **The less said about it, the better.** Sucking may gradually subside, especially if no special attention is given to reinforce it.
2. **Avoid using the child's name** in reference to thumb-sucking. "Disconnect" the child's identity from sucking behavior.
3. **Give ample nourishment.** Replace thumb-sucking with breast, bottle, or cup feeding, depending on the child's stage.
4. **If the child is still thumb- or finger-sucking near the end of the second year,** you might use the upcoming third birthday as a way to help the child end this habit. For example, say, "You are soon going to be three years old. What a big girl you're about to be. Now you can let go of your two-year-old thumb-sucking habit. You can simply stop sucking your thumb. Can you do this yourself, or do you need me to help you?"

Using Swear Words

A mother told about her son who began to swear when he was about five years old. She tried a variety of ways to help him stop, but she was unsuccessful. Finally, one day she told him, "You will have to leave home if you keep using those words." For a couple of days, he didn't use any "bad" words, but then came the day. So she said, "Go, pack your bags. You will have to leave because we cannot have those bad words spoken in our family." She watched him take his backpack and walk down the hill from their house. She began to worry, of course, as a mother would. So she got in her car and drove down the hill. There he was, sitting at the bottom of the hill on a rock ledge. She got out, sat down beside him, and asked, "Where are you going?" He replied, "Gosh, Mom, I don't know where in the hell to go." She said, "Get in; let's go home."

Threats and bribes won't help a child break a habit. We need to help children learn new patterns of behavior. If a child is using profanity, we need to give examples of appropriate words. Then we need to model these in a sentence and have the child find words that can take the place of "bad" words.

A good way to help a child is to state, "We use *regular* words in our house," or, "We use *school* words at school."

It's helpful to tell the child that *slang*, or *pejoratives*, is unacceptable. Then say to the child, "Do you know what a pejorative is?" The younger child likely will not know. Then explain that we use words we know, and when we get angry or upset, we can simply say, "I am really angry," or, "I am upset." When dealing with a preschooler, we can talk about getting rid of slang or pejoratives by imagining they are thrown out the window and they fly away with the wind. Or, ask the child how he or she would pretend to get rid of these words.

Temper Tantrums

Most children, from time to time, express their feelings with temper tantrums. These outbursts are usually spontaneous, in an instant, with total loss of impulse control by the child. In most cases, a child who has a temper tantrum has been trying to gain control of someone else. When that doesn't work, the child loses self-control, and the tantrum is the result. Some tantrums last no longer than a few seconds, while others seem to go on forever.

What to Do about a Tantrum

The adult who remains calm generally makes good progress in handling temper tantrums. Most children calm themselves when given the opportunity. However, parents and teachers often want to act in order to stop a tantrum. Each case is a little different, so you have to decide what is best when you face this challenge. Here are a few suggestions:

- Stoop down, and in a calm voice, ask the child, "What is it that you want?" There is rarely a child who won't stop the tantrum and tell you. It may take several seconds for the child to calm down enough to say what he or she wants. Then talk with the child about these wishes. After the child has calmed down, you can usually help the child move toward appropriate behavior. When children have the opportunity to talk about what they want, that's often enough to satisfy them, even when they can't have their way.

- When the child is out of control, and the above suggestion doesn't work, simply remove the audience. Say to the child, "Go ahead and have your tantrum, but I won't watch you. When you finish, we can talk." Then turn your back for about fifteen seconds.

- When in the company of others, pick the child up, and carry him or her out of the room or place. Put the child down gently, and give permission to express feelings: "Go ahead and cry, and let your feelings out. Then we can talk." When the child settles down, then you can talk and take proper steps to solve the problem. When you carry a child out of the presence of others, always say to those remaining, "I am taking him out so he can express his feelings without disturbing you. I am not going to hurt him."

In some cases, you and other children or siblings can leave the room where the tantrum is going on. In this case, let the others know what to expect, such as, "She needs to get her feelings out, so let's go outdoors. When she has settled, she can join us."

Power Struggles

Children naturally have a need to be in control. They will sometimes go to extreme behaviors to gain control in certain situations. We most often experience this need when a child engages an adult in a power struggle. When this occurs, the adult has the upper hand as the mature person in the struggle. For one thing, adults are viewed as "authority figures. They know best; they are bigger and stronger; they are in charge." As long as the adult keeps in mind this is how the child perceives the adult, the power struggle will subside.

Many times, the power struggle becomes a challenge for the child to hold out as long as possible to gain control. *If I keep on crying and screaming, she will surely give up and let me have my way.* Such thought on the child's part adds energy to continue the struggle. The adult who is willing to work through the struggle with the child, regardless of the time it takes, will be successful in helping the child learn that "this limit is real," or "she means what she says." It may take twenty minutes or more to get through the struggle, but it will be worth the time and effort. You can help by practicing some of the following suggestions.

1. **Remain calm.** The child is out of control; you are in control. Your disposition will help the child settle down sooner than if you lose your composure.
2. **Avoid using the child's name.** Give as little recognition to the child as possible.
3. **Direct your comments toward the child's situation.** Let the child know you care about what happens to him. For example, three-year-old Sandra refused to take a nap because she wanted both her own stuffed toy and her sister's. Her sister was ready to sleep but wanted her own toy for cuddling. The power struggle was launched as Sandra held on tight to both toys. Her mom tried to disengage them, explaining that her sister is entitled to her own toy. In such a case, try these kinds of action:

    *   Take the toy from her, even though this may require using physical force to pry it loose. Say, "Your sister may have her toy. You and I are going to leave the room and deal with this problem." Then take the child out and say, "I am not going to hurt you. We are going to talk about this." The child may be screaming all the way, kicking, and crying. That is to be expected. Remain calm—this, too, shall pass.
    *   Give the child permission to be angry and disappointed, to cry or scream, as long as no one gets hurt. Say, "You may scream as long as you need to. You may cry and throw a fit. When you are ready to settle down, we will talk about it.
    *   Be prepared to let the child scream, cry, and show anger. Keep your own voice calm, yet firm. "When you can settle down and get yourself together, we will talk about this." You may have to suggest from time to time that the child is ready to stop crying. "I think you are ready to stop crying and talk. Tell me what you would like to do." The child may settle enough to say, "I want both cuddlies." Crying may then begin a new cycle. That's all right. Give permission, but stay with it. Say to the child, "I know you *wish* you could have both cuddlies. I wish

you could have both." This gives the child the message that you understand and care.

- When the child has expressed enough feelings and is settled enough to talk, let her say whatever she needs to. You must then be prepared to continue to hold the position that her sister is entitled to her own toy, just as she is. If the tantrum recycles, so be it. You must be prepared to stay with it. Again, give the child permission to express feelings. "Go ahead and cry and get all your angry feelings out. I will wait as long as I have to for you to finish. Then we will talk about it."

- The child will finally settle down. Then you can say, "I think you are ready to go in and take your rest. Here you may have your toy." At this point, offer to give the child a hug, saying, "Here, let's have a big hug." When the hug occurs, you will sense that the child is relaxed. Then you can say with confidence, "You have your cuddly, and your sister has hers. I will go with you and help you get settled." Take the child by the hand gently back to the bed and continue. You will be pleased, even though exhausted, and your child will know that parents are concerned about helping their children when things get out of hand. There is great comfort for the child in knowing that if her sister took her toy, you would step in and return it. This builds trust between parent and child and gives the message that limits are real.

Sibling Rivalry

Having a new baby in the family is one of the most exciting events in a lifetime. The anticipation of a baby brother or sister brings delight to most young children. Their fantasies flourish, and they imagine wonderful times together. When the baby arrives, it's like having a new toy, something unlike anything before. Then the scenario changes. After a few weeks or months, the older child begins to think something like, I'm not sure about this new baby stuff. I sure have to give up a lot of attention from my parents. I think we better send the baby back.

Parents begin to see signals that indicate the older sibling is feeling deprived and hurt. But this is natural and to be expected. After all, when a child has been on the throne three or four years and then takes a fall, it hurts. The child may begin to feel resentment and attempt to express these feelings by pinching or hurting the baby. Some children speak directly about their feelings, while others dramatize them.

Helping Children Adapt
Most children get through their periods of resentment and feelings of deprivation after about six or eight weeks. During this time, however, parents can expect such behaviors as:

- Regression in toilet training
- Thumb-sucking, or even wanting a bottle again
- Temper tantrums
- Oppositional behavior, especially toward adults
- Clinging to the parent

These behaviors are usually an attempt on the part of the child to get in fantasy what cannot be accomplished in reality. The child's notion is that, *If I can be little again, there won't be anyone else. I will get all the attention and won't have to share my time.* Some children fantasize that a new baby is going to be like a new toy—when you get tired of it, just get rid of it. When they discover this is not possible, they feel the pain of facing reality.

We can understand how the older child must feel since independence and a sense of self, still forming, has suddenly been disrupted. The entrance of a new baby with the shift in attention is more than most young children can cope with unless they have help.

There are several ways adults can help children get ready for a new baby while giving reassurance, love, and affection:

- **Talk with the child a few weeks in advance of the baby's birth.** Be receptive to the child's reaction and questions, as these will give clues about how the child feels and what thoughts are emerging in the child's mind.
- **Respond to questions and comments with simple statements.** This will help the child grasp the idea of what it will be like to have a new baby in the family. Even though the expectant

sibling may not fully understand the permanence of the new family member, there will be an element of excitement about the situation. Answer only the questions asked in a simple and factual way. Elaboration is not necessary and may only cloud the situation. Keep the door open for additional concerns when the child is ready.

- **Continue to give affection and attention in the usual manner.** When parents give more love and attention than usual, they may set the child up for greater disappointment later when time has to be shared with the baby.
- **Prepare the child by sharing stories, books, and play about getting ready for a new baby.** Use puppets and dolls for role-playing to give the child opportunities to express worries and feelings as well as to express excitement about this upcoming event.
- **Talk with your child about what it is like to be a baby.** Look at baby pictures from the family album. Let the child taste baby food and explore baby toys.

When the Baby Arrives

This first day or two will be filled with excitement and joy. After that, watch out! There may be a sudden change in the older child because this transition time is being made out of necessity and not out of choice. While some children go through the transition of a new baby with little difficulty, others tend to turn the family upside down. Because every child is unique, parents need to be alert to children's patterns for coping. Consider these suggestions in helping make transitions:

- Set aside special time with the older child to do things together, without the baby.
- Include the older child in activities with the baby, taking cues about how much is enough. Some children begin to feel like "servants" when expected to do too many tasks as the parent's helper.
- When friends and relatives are present, be sure to focus on the older child as well as on the newborn. There is a natural tendency for visitors to give their attention to the new baby, and the older sibling soon begins to feel left out.

- Encourage the child to play with the baby, but again, take the cues about how much is joyful and how much is painful.

Children Learn about Being Siblings

Most children enjoy learning about babies. They can express their feelings—good or bad—while engaging in this new experience. Help children accept and enjoy their roles as siblings by developing the following concepts.

- Babies are fragile and are to be handled carefully, supporting their heads and touching them gently.
- The word "attachment" means looking into the baby's eyes and talking or singing, touching, and giving gentle affection.
- Babies can't do for themselves, and they depend on others for health and safety.
- Babies giggle and coo—and cry—as a way of communicating.

Children learn more about themselves as they live with siblings. They are curious and want to know about babies. Children, like babies, also are intrigued by their body movements, vocalizations, and facial expressions. Even a two-year-old feels "grown up" in comparison to the baby in the family.

Sibling Interactions

Sibling rivalry is viewed by some as a behavior to be changed. However, this rivalry is not only natural; it is necessary. Children learn to negotiate and develop the art of communication by interacting in the home setting. This behavior provides opportunities to learn give-and-take, sharing, standing one's ground, handling disappointments, and the joy of sibling attachments.

Children usually do best with each other when there is little interference from parents or other adults. Children naturally learn to get along and to work through their differences. They need to "bump up against" one another in order to learn that others have their own unique characteristics.

Intervention is most effective when it promotes respect. Adults who step in to prevent harmful behavior can help children learn that freedom comes with a sense of responsibility for respectful behavior. The four **rules of respect** previously discussed also help safeguard sibling safety while promoting caring attitudes and self-control:

- Respect for self
- Respect for others
- Respect for property
- Respect for nature

Most siblings engage in a variety of testing behaviors with one another, including competition, threats or commands, and verbal and physical altercations. These are all natural. When push comes to shove, most siblings take up for one another. Their love and attachment is usually strong enough to outweigh their rivalry. But isn't it a positive feeling to know that most siblings practice their social skills at home with one another and then apply these appropriately in public?

Resolving Conflicts
Play is an ideal way for children to learn to resolve conflict. They learn to get along by being together, by having to share and cooperate. Play frees them to express feelings of disagreement, to change directions and negotiate a settlement without losing face. Children may come to some form of resolution or adaptation even when the problem itself cannot be solved. Sometimes they cry, scream, yell, and mope; other times they simply shrug and go forward. Many times children settle their differences without the awareness of parents and teachers.

Parents who maintain respect for each other, even when disagreeing, demonstrate the value of human dignity and worth. Children who see this behavior learn to get along, to compromise, and to see another person's point of view. Most of all, they learn that conflict and disagreement are a part of the real world.

Children of all ages *benefit* from arguments and disagreements with parents, even when both get angry and upset. Such experiences help children build trust in their relationships. Children who trust their parents enough to throw a tantrum or engage in disagreement are able to test the limits without fear of severe punishment. Yet they also learn that differences can be resolved without acting out. Many parent-child relationships become stronger after conflicts have been resolved. This is especially true when adults are willing to listen to children's views and ideas—even when they don't approve.

My Sister's Birth

I sadly watched Dad move out my stuff from my room that I loved
    so badly and was mad because my new sister was born.
I had to move to an old creepy room upstairs, and told my parents
    that I was scared that the floors creaked and so did the stairs.
She cried every day and woke up in the middle of the night.
Mom tried to comfort her and to hold her tight;
she had a soft smile and smelled like fresh powder.
I heard the water on from the shower,
and it scared my sister later, and I
comforted her,
and I decided I liked her after all.

—Courtney L. Crawford

Bully Behavior

The *bully* feels inadequate and powerless to solve problems or gain satisfaction in socially appropriate ways. Being pushy and exercising physical aggression is a way to send an external signal about an internal feeling.

Bullies are not usually violent. Their bullying behaviors are natural ways to use their bodies and their words in attempts to solve problems or gain attention. Most bullies have misperceptions about themselves. They may think of themselves as ugly, not very smart, rejected, or unimportant. They become desperate and begin compensating for such feelings of inadequacy by *succeeding as a "bad kid."*

Even though it may be hurtful to others, physical attack is also a way of making contact. It is a way of getting the victim's attention. Bully behavior usually means, "I want you to like me, or notice me—I want to feel important."

The Bully-Victim Cycle

On the other hand, there would be no bullies if there were no *victims*. Some children always seem to be victims. Habitual victims usually lack self-confidence and self-respect. They are often children whose parents are overprotective and tend to come to a child's rescue during the early years. Consequently, the child does not learn to face challenges of the real world. Then, when the child goes to school or off to play, he or she is vulnerable to attack by the bully who senses and exploits the child's weakness.

When we can look back into the early years of bullies, we often discover that they had poor attachments with one or both parents. That is, they may have been abused or neglected by one or both parents. One parent may have left the family when the child was under four or five years old. These children feel less secure than those who experienced trusting relationships with their parents. Even in one-parent families, many children develop self-confidence and feel good about themselves because they have a loving parent who gives consistent care and affection during their early years. These children rarely become bullies. They have inner strength, and the bully senses their self-assurance and leaves them alone. The bully approaches those who appear to be vulnerable and weak.

Looking back into the early years of children who become victims, we generally discover they also had poor attachments, but not in the same way as the bullies. The victims often had parents who were unsure of themselves, did not feel comfortable as parents, and were often absent from their children. These children grew up with fears of rejection and abandonment. They also feared whether or not their parents would return after being absent. While these parents were not abusive, they lacked the consistent presence and care that makes young children feel secure. Divorced or separated parents are often preoccupied with personal problems and may fail to give the support that growing children need in order to develop with a sense of self-assurance.

In rare cases, some bully behavior becomes serious and extreme. A bully who is very troubled may seek out victims who cannot protect themselves, such as young children. Or, a bully may attack a group of people or an individual who does not expect to be involved in violent behavior. This kind of violent bully behavior is unusual and not the same as most bully behavior. However, all bully behavior is unacceptable. The best way to stop this behavior is to prevent it by helping children develop a strong sense of self-confidence. Parents who are closely connected, or attached, to their children from the time they are born generally provide a safe and comfortable environment for children to grow and learn. Children who are secure have no need to be bullies and no desire to be victims.

Violence and Crime

Perhaps we must take a closer look at what is occurring when youths use knives and guns to solve their problems or express their feelings. These acts of violence may be *metaphors* that reflect deep-seated feelings and disruptions of rational thinking. Perhaps the child is "cutting out" or "stabbing to death" that which is so painful or repulsive. The child may be performing emotional surgery on a "cancer of the spirit" that is felt within his or her own life.

Many children act in concrete ways to solve abstract problems. They seek immediate relief because they have little or no basis for *delayed gratification*. The stability of trust and self-confidence makes it possible for a child to tolerate waiting for satisfaction or relief from what is unpleasant. But without this emotional stability, a child is vulnerable to taking the quickest action for relief from pain or for getting what brings immediate satisfaction—even when the child knows better.

"Blowing someone away" is a quick means to stop emotional pain. A youth kills to eliminate the threat of being killed by trauma or perceived deprivation. Guns and knives represent sources of power. Children often feel powerless to do anything about the inner emotional agony they experience. But with the external power from guns and knives, they have an immediate means to terminate that internal pain or emotional sickness they feel inside. They imagine violence as a solution without thinking about what comes next.

Unfortunately, violent and criminal acts are committed by children and adolescents as well as by adults. Many of these youths are smart. They are creative thinkers, and they gain satisfaction from outsmarting the law and their victims. Others act out of fear and desperation and without regard for possible consequences. Still others are influenced by peer pressure and the need to feel important and accepted.

Common Elements among Youths Who Break the Law

There are some elements that can be found among the children and adolescents who commit violent acts and who break the law.

Needs are not being met through appropriate behaviors:

- A need to belong to a group
- A desire to be viewed as important
- The motivation to achieve success
- A need for safety and protection
- A desire to make a contribution to a group
- The need for satisfaction from hunger and shelter

When these needs are met by the family, school, and community in positive ways, children generally feel secure, successful, and important. However, when children view themselves as inadequate in the eyes of parents, teachers, and peers, they may seek ways to gain success, even if it means being a "successful law-breaker."

The inability to delay gratification:

- A strong desire to get immediate satisfaction
- A lack of trust in parents that personal needs will be met

Children who grow up with close attachments to parents and lots of love usually develop a strong *sense of trust.* Conversely, children who feel estranged or rejected by parents may have little basis for building trust. Let's review three parenting styles that help to illustrate how children either learn trust and delayed gratification, or grow up seeking it.

Parenting Styles Influence Behavior

1. **Neglectful parent behavior.** Some parents are unable or unwilling to meet the needs of their babies. When an infant cries and yearns for ten or fifteen minutes or more and is not attended, that child feels neglected. The child's message is, "I need help," "I'm hungry," or, "Please play with me." If the neglect continues on a regular basis, the child may grow up to be a teenager who thinks, *I may as*

well get what I need or want any way I can because there is no one who cares.

2. **Overindulgent parent behavior.** Some parents are overprotective and bend over backward to give their children everything they think they need or want. For example, some parents check the baby continually to be sure the diapers are dry, wake the baby for feedings, give the baby lots to eat and drink, and carry the baby most of the time—even when the child is capable of walking. Overindulged children have no need to build trust because they never have to wait. They don't even have to alert someone when they are in need. Many of these babies grow into childhood without awareness of having needs. If overindulgence continues, children may grow up thinking, *I want it, and I want it now! I've always gotten what I want, and I shouldn't have to wait. I refuse to wait; I'll just get it any way I can.*

3. **Mutually caring parent behavior.** Parents who generate mutual, or sharing, relationships with their children are helping to build trust. For example, when their babies cry, some parents respond within a few minutes, but they don't stumble over themselves to get there. When the baby waits a few minutes to have needs met, the sense is, "When I'm hungry, they always feed me, even if I cry a little." Or, "I can count on them to come to my rescue, even if I have to wait a while." These babies soon learn, by waiting a short time, that someone can be expected to meet their needs. This helps children view themselves as separate individuals from their parents, yet secure with them. Even as infants, they sense they have "power" to get help or attention. They also know it's all right to wait. When mutual relationships continue, children grow into adolescence thinking, *I may have to wait to get what I want or need, but they have always come through,* or, *I can wait; it won't be the end of the world.*

We can see that in all three of the above examples of parenting styles, children quickly learn what to expect and what they can count on. Some decide to act in their own way to get what they need or want—even when they know it is against the law.

Violence as an Act of Fear or Desperation

Violent behavior is often the result of fear. Preteens and adolescents become nervous and desperate when they think their lives are in danger. They often shoot first even if it means killing someone. Their thinking is, *If I don't get them first, they will kill me.* They also fear being caught unless they eliminate their victims.

Even the smartest children make mistakes. When fear escalates, rational judgment diminishes. Some children lose sight of what they are doing and simply act out of fear.

Acting Out in Retaliation

Children who are abused learn to abuse others. This may be expected as a natural way of life. These children think that's the way things are supposed to be. Hitting and beating are ways to control others. Children also may seek revenge and retaliate to "get even."

Crime and Violence as a Way of Life

Much of the violence and crime in densely populated areas is a result of learning from others. Gangs and packs of youths have strong leaders. They know how to get guns, knives, and other weapons. Belonging to a gang means living up to certain "standards." This may mean stealing, killing, and torturing people.

Going to jail often becomes a status symbol. This is a place to see how the "meanest" rule the cells and the inside activities. Youths emulate their idols by the clothes they wear, hairdos, and speech patterns. When these youths get out of jail, they are more experienced and often become gang or cult leaders themselves.

Life Has Little Meaning

Children who grow up in neighborhoods where crime and violence are common tend to view street wars, drug traffic, stealing, beatings, and killings as everyday activity. Life often is cut short for many people they know. They learn quickly to look out for themselves. Their need to survive motivates them to arm themselves. Their sense is, *It's better to kill than to be killed.* Experiencing violence year after year conditions young children to view life as having little meaning—or not much chance for a future.

The children are smart. They are simply living out the patterns of behavior they have learned since childhood. Many of them learn how to evade the law, or how to "get the most out of being caught." They become "famous within the community of law-breakers. They often have good leadership ability and a keen sense of how to interact with others to get what they want.

Victims May Encourage Violence and Crime
Children and adults who feel helpless to protect themselves are often targets for aggressive and highly motivated youths. Some children tend to assume roles as victims, especially when they have been either overprotected or neglected by parents during their early years of childhood. Victims often thrive on fear and are easily threatened by those looking for a fight or to take advantage of someone. Elderly and disabled people often are attacked, and even killed, by youths who are afraid to leave a witness to their crimes and violence.

Suicide
Unfortunately, children and adolescents are not immune to such a tragedy as suicide. Those who contemplate or attempt suicide are usually troubled and see only one option to solving a problem or resolving certain issues. Whether the notion of suicide is premeditated or impulsive, it reflects a child's feelings of desperation and hopelessness. When children talk about taking their own lives or wishing they were dead, we need to listen carefully and respond with understanding rather than ridicule.

There are usually indications that something is seriously troubling a person prior to such action as either a threat or an attempt to take one's own life. Some leave notes or writings in hopes that someone will find them. Others make comments that reflect they see only one way "out." Some reflect a dramatic change in behavior. These are usually calls for help that indicate children and adolescents need someone they can trust and confide in during critical times. While many suicides are unsuspected by family and friends, there are often signals that go unnoticed. When parents or teachers are concerned about a child, getting help may prevent a tragedy.

When a child says, "I'm just going to kill myself," someone needs to take notice and do something to discover options for helping this person. Notes are also important clues that a child is troubled. Children and adolescents usually leave these where they know someone will see them. Some students tell others they are depressed and want to commit suicide. They need help. Even when this is just another way to get attention, it is also a clue that the person has a problem and needs help.

Gangs and Cults Use Rituals to Strengthen Bonding

Ritual plays a major role in helping children feel safe and satisfied. As humans, we share a basic need to participate in rituals. The *old brain* in the human seeks satisfaction from repeating ceremonial, or ritualistic, practices.

Gangs, or peer groups, have been a part of every society. Children have a natural tendency to want to belong to a social group because part of the human brain seeks satisfaction from *connecting with other humans*. When children participate in family and community rituals, they feel a sense of satisfaction and stability. When there is no ritual at home, many children gravitate toward gangs.

Families and school programs can provide satisfaction for their children by engaging in rituals as a regular practice. For example, children who participate in evening meals at home with their families have opportunities to talk and share ideas and feelings. When they feel important, they look forward to each day's evening meal. Another example is the family that celebrates certain holidays by preparing a meal or special foods, decorating, dressing in costumes, and celebrating with music and joyful activities. Such events give attention to children and provide ways for them to feel important in the eyes of their parents and relatives. There is a close bonding between family members who do things together on a regular basis. Children look forward to these events and enjoy preparing and participating.

Religious groups generally practice ritual in their ceremonies and meetings. Many children experience these rituals with their families, while some children and youths attend on their own.

On the other hand, children who do not experience rituals at home or in school or the community may gravitate toward gangs or cults that offer these practices. While they may not be aware of the power of ritualistic practices in certain gangs and cults, young people may be attracted to the false sense of satisfaction they experience. Most gangs that engage in violent or unlawful acts have organized rituals that must be followed by each member. This gives the member a sense of belonging, of being important, of making a contribution, and of being accepted. Even if the ritual includes bringing proof of having harmed someone, it offers a challenge to connect with a group that promises to protect and satisfy—even when these are false promises.

Gangs and cults always have ritual. It's an important part of the gangs' and cults' stability. Ritual is something that a person can count on. It helps to bring about bonding. Gangs that engage in violent or unlawful behaviors practice rituals that fit into their goals for membership. Certain clothing styles, language patterns, and symbolic behaviors often add to the power of a gang's or cult's identity.

What is important is that children are attracted to "the group" that offers them ways to get their needs met and for them to feel that someone really cares about them. Children who find safety and satisfaction in their families or school and community groups generally take on the values of these groups. By the same token, children who go outside the family to participate in unlawful gang or cult activities often take up the values of these groups.

Children who find satisfaction through ritual in their own families are not as tempted to seek gang or cult membership. But parents also can pick up on clues about their children's interests by noticing their habit patterns of going out at certain times, dressing in a particular manner, and failing to talk about where they have been and who their friends are.

Runaways and Human Trafficking

International human trafficking (taking people against their will) has become the fastest-growing criminal enterprise in the world. Unfortunately, thousands of young people in America and other countries, especially teenage girls, are being caught up in the traps that move them to various parts of the world for exploitation as prostitutes, sexual entertainers, slave workers, and beggars.

Many of the victims of human trafficking are girls who run away from home. Some are on drugs, some are defiant toward parents, and some simply want to be away for a while. However, many of these girls are picked up and drugged or starved to make them submit to exploitation. After three days of being deprived of food, or after becoming addicted to drugs, most of these victims will do anything to get relief. They often are promised safety, protection, and love—all empty promises by their captors. Once they have been shipped to a foreign country, or held in captivity in their own country, they face the peril of a lifetime of trauma.

Heading Off Violence and Crime

Parents and teachers can do more than anyone else to prevent youths from engaging in violence and crime, or becoming victims of crime. Knowing that children are smart and that they have common needs, there are several ways to help children grow and develop as responsible and respectful individuals.

First, we must keep in mind, the goals most parents share are similar for all children as they develop their character. These goals include:

- Self-confidence
- Interdependence
- Caring and respectful attitudes
- Responsible behavior
- Active learning
- Creative expression
- A close bonding and attachment with parents

Second, we can be aware of each child's sense of self-worth, especially in the eyes of parents, teachers, and peers. Children look first to adults for getting their physical and emotional needs met. We must be there to help meet their needs so they feel worthwhile. When personal needs are met, children don't feel pulled toward inappropriate ways of getting satisfaction.

Take an active interest in what happens to children. The following adult actions will enable most children to engage in appropriate behaviors that reflect respect and regard for themselves and others. Caring parents practice these every day:

1. Treat every child with concern and respect.
2. Talk with children to understand what they think and how they feel.

3. Listen with a caring ear—even when disagreement occurs.
4. Engage children in establishing rules and limits.
5. Enforce consequences when limits and rules are violated.
6. Encourage children to participate in a wide range of activities with realistic expectations and outcomes.
7. Insist that schools provide high-quality education with outstanding teachers, and get involved to help make this possible.

Nurturance Rather than Dominance

Children who experience plenty of support from family and friends generally feel a sense of stability. The support they need comes from genuine interest in them, and in what they think and how they feel—as well as what they do or want to do.

Recently, I was in a conversation with a woman while I visited relatives. When I asked about her work, she said, "I teach the children from hell." After gasping and getting hold of my teeth, I asked her to tell me about her experiences. She said the children were from outrageous home situations; they were often truant, unruly, and mean, and sometimes vicious. After a lengthy visit, she said, "What can I do? I'm desperate. I can't afford to retire yet, and I hate to abandon these kids." So we talked over her options.

She agreed that these children were not retarded or slow learners, even though they were placed in a class for "remediation." The approach we worked on was to capitalize on the talents of one of the leaders, a fourteen-year-old boy who was always getting himself and others into trouble and who never did his classwork.

The following steps were developed, and over the semester, she began to see positive results.

1. View the boy with compassion—love without attachment.
2. Talk with him privately, and let him know that he is respected as a person. For example, say: "While I don't approve of your behavior in here, I do like you as a person. I notice that you have a real talent for attracting other kids and for getting them to do whatever you say. That tells me you have a lot of person-power.

What a personality you have! You know, I'd like to get you on my side because you seem to succeed at every turn in getting the kids in here to do what you want. What's your secret? When you're in the mood, I'd like us to talk. I want to know you better—I want to know what makes you tick."

3. Develop a relationship that keeps his behavior in proper perspective. "Like I said, while I do not approve of your behavior in here, I do like you, and I'm glad you're in my class. Let's talk about how we can work together. You seem to work magic as a leader. How do you do it?"

4. Help him establish reachable goals that will reflect his abilities and bring him success in school. "Tell me, if you could do anything in the world, what would you do? I'm interested in your ideas. What are your dreams—what do you imagine yourself being?" Listen to him, and then help translate his ideas and wishes into realistic and appropriate possibilities.

5. Keep communications open, and listen to his personal woes if he wishes to share them. Help him interpret his own message in a way that has meaning for him. Encourage him to suggest ways to convert his energy from "emotional garbage" into energy for academic achievement. Open the door for sharing, but let him come through when he is ready.

6. Help him build self-confidence as a responsible student by giving positive feedback. Use his name when he does what is acceptable, and avoid his name when he misbehaves so that he begins to behave appropriately to get recognition.

7. Ask his advice on how to handle the other students. When the advice is sound, use it—and let him know you appreciate it.

8. Work with integrity and confidence. Be genuine and realistic because he will know if you're faking.

Even the most difficult student yearns for an adult who is open to listening and caring. Teachers often serve as a lifeline without which some students might never make it—in school or in life. In rare cases, a lifeline can mean planning a future rather than planning a funeral.

Support Comes to Children in Many Ways

- Playing with children
- Reading to young children
- Going places and doing things together
- Talking with children about what is important to them
- Listening to children's concerns and problems—and to their wishes and dreams
- Expressing genuine interest in their ideas and asking their advice, especially about issues that relate directly to them
- Mutually giving and sharing
- Expressing love and affection in a variety of ways

Pain and Anguish

In my heart
I feel a pain,
pain of loss
that I never had.
When I see what I could have held,
I see a dark hand covers my face,
blinding my sight in the night
where the face is wiped from the light.

I feel my soul burn
as if hell's fire covers my mind.
My loss is not your loss
but the loss of love.
When I see you go down the path
that I cannot follow
I feel despair and anguish
over the loss that I can never have.

I am in pain
so much of my life.
Why does it give me
such suffering and strife?
I have every problem

you could think.
Smoking, drugs and things to drink.
Things that screw with your mind,
but they feel so good when you're
in such a bind.
A bind such as this
can never be cured.
But I wish they could all be burned.

—A young teenager

CHAPTER 7

Behavioral Disorders

A serious behavioral problem that disrupts a child's normal development is usually a condition that calls for professional help. To distinguish a disorder from a common behavior, one must be able to document a *recurring problem* that does one of these things:

- Persists over several months.
- Appears to be getting consistently worse or shows no sign of improvement.
- Tends to interfere with the child's ability to get along with others or to perform simple tasks.
- Reflects violent, aggressive, or hurtful acts toward others or oneself on a consistent basis.

Be Alert to Children's Signals

Many children are smart enough to mask, or hide, the underlying feelings and perceptions that can bring about serious problems or disorders.

They often give signals that "all is not well," but they rarely will ask for help. Many children don't actually realize they have problems, yet their behaviors usually give clues. Even the smartest children may have misperceptions, or incorrect ideas, about how others view them. Some children even imagine that teachers or peers don't accept them. So when troubled children say they don't have anything to talk about, they may be sending out a call for help. For some, what is going on in their lives may "hurt too much" to talk about.

The *Diagnostic and Statistical Manual of Mental Disorders* is a reference published by the American Psychiatric Association. Every few years, an updated version is published. The latest is referred to as the DSM-5, published in 2013.

The priority goal of this manual is to provide a guide to clinical practice. This guide is designed for use by psychiatrists, other physicians, psychologists, social workers, nurses, occupational and rehab therapists, counselors, and other health and mental health professionals. Research and statistics are an ongoing part of revisions of this publication. This is not a guide for use by parents or people without training in its application. However, parents aware of this resource will be better able to communicate with professionals when their children are diagnosed. Generally, when a professional gives a diagnosis for a child or adolescent, it will be in one of two forms:

1. **Categorical:** A number and title are recorded in the professional record. (Example: 315.39 Language Disorder) (For professional use.)
2. **Functional:** Difficulties in communication involving both verbal language (written and spoken) and sign language. These difficulties interfere with academic or occupational achievement, or with social communications. (For use in communicating with parents about the child's diagnosis.)

Some of the more common disorders that parents may suspect in their children, and that require professional diagnosis, are important to consider. However, because children are smart, they may be able to imitate others or reflect elements of disorders that are simply misbehaviors.

Awareness is the key to recognizing symptoms or signs that indicate a serious disorder.

Autism spectrum disorder is characterized by severe difficulties in a child's ability to communicate in social settings and to understand relationships. These children often have patterns of behavior that are repeated over and over. They have difficulty getting along with others, sharing feelings and thoughts, and carrying on social conversations. They may exhibit strict adherence to routines and resistance to change. These types of behaviors persist over long periods of time, even months and years. Parents concerned about the possibility of a child having autism will be wise to consult with a professional for a diagnosis and then for therapy. There is guidance available to suggest ways parents can help their children.

The term **attention deficit/hyperactivity disorder (ADHD)** is the designated diagnosis for children who display symptoms that are often called hyperactivity and that persist for at least six months. A child with ADHD consistently reflects:

- A short attention span—an inability to stay on task
- Poor concentration, impulsive outbursts—an inability to wait
- Overactivity and "out of control" behavior—an inability to stay seated
- An increasing history of school failure—makes careless mistakes
- A lack of persistence—difficulty focusing
- An inability to get along with peers—intruding into others' activities

Parents or teachers who suspect that a child has ADHD need to keep observation notes of the child's behaviors. Write a brief description of what the child does, and write the date and time of day on the notation. Keep a log of the observations to see whether or not the above symptoms are consistent over several weeks. In addition to keeping the log, consider the following questions:

1. Has the child had these symptoms for at least six months?
2. Did these symptoms begin before age seven?

3. Is the child's behavior very different from most other children of the same age range?
4. Is the child unable to sit or be still, even when he or she *wants* to be still?
5. Does the child have great difficulty following through with instructions, even though he or she understands them?
6. Does the child continuously fidget or squirm, moving hands, feet, or the whole body?

If your answer is consistently *yes* to all these questions, then talk with the teacher. If you *are* the teacher, talk with the parent, and consult the school psychologist or counselor. Or suggest to parents that a referral be made for an evaluation by a child psychiatrist, physician, or psychologist.

Disruptive, impulse-control, and conduct disorders involve problems of self-control of emotions and behaviors. The child seems to have no sense of control from within. These behaviors include aggression, destruction of property, and conflict with social rules and authority figures. A small percentage of children may be diagnosed with a conduct disorder that is characterized by a consistent pattern of bullying, cruelty toward other children, and physical attacks on peers. These children have few or no friends. Many children are afraid of them or don't know how to interact with them. Professional help is needed to diagnose children with severe disruptive behaviors, a lack of impulse control, and conduct disorders.

Oppositional defiant disorder is characterized by a consistent pattern of behavior that reflects:

- Arguing with others, including parents and peers
- An irritable mood, anger, and vindictiveness
- Annoying others on purpose
- Cursing and yelling when things don't go "my way"
- A refusal to follow rules and limits
- A loss of temper, especially with parents and other adults

These behaviors must last at least six months and occur with at least one person who is not a sibling. These children eventually may have anxiety and depressive disorders, but they don't usually develop conduct disorders.

Again, these behaviors must be observed over a long period of time to reflect a disorder. Many children engage in misbehaviors from time to time, but unless they are continuous, they are generally acts of natural defiance against authority or a test of children's own sense of self.

Troubled Children, Troubled Families

Troubled families often have troubled children. These children tend to worry about what is going on, especially when they feel helpless to do anything to help. Family problems often become "psychological baggage" that children carry with them. It is as though they are "carrying heavy bags" that weigh them down.

In order to keep communication open, watch for these signals that something may be worrying a child or interfering with schoolwork:

- A sudden resistance to performing school tasks
- Incomplete homework or class assignments
- A lack of animated, or spontaneous, facial expressions
- Body language that says "I'm tired" all the time
- Frequent use of such phrases as "I can't" or "Who cares?"
- Obvious misbehaviors that begin to be repeated

Take this grade school child as an example. Tim usually behaved appropriately and then suddenly had an outburst when his teacher asked him a question. Similar behavior, while not acceptable, did occur from time to time with other students and was therefore overlooked as possibly serious for Tim. However, Tim began to have other inappropriate behaviors. The teacher became concerned that there might be some unresolved feelings or issues that needed attention. After class at the end of the week, Tim's teacher talked privately with him about his behaviors. Tim burst into tears and poured out his feelings about his dad moving away.

Talking with Children

Talking with children often helps them know that you are aware they may be having strong feelings about something that is bothering them. You may be able to keep the way open for talking by simply making a statement such as:

- "It seems to me you're worried about something."
- "You are usually quite excited about participating in class, but I've noticed that lately you are very quiet."
- "Sometimes I bet you wish things were different in your life."
- "Anytime you feel like talking about what's bothering you, I'm interested in what you have to say."

These responses may be accompanied by drooped shoulders and head, poor eye contact, and a weak voice tone—or shouting. Some children drop their books or slam them down, as if to send a message such as, "Can't you see that I'm upset?"

Keep the invitation open for talking, but avoid being pushy. For example, say: "I just want you to know that I think your ideas—and your feelings—are important. I'll be interested if you decide you want to talk."

While some children may not respond immediately, they may come around to talk when they feel ready.

Feelings of helplessness can be disabling, as if a child were physically injured. He "chokes" on the bitterness between family members that is too tough to swallow.

CHAPTER 8

Living with
a Smart Child

Be flexible, and you will survive. Adults face a unique task in relating effectively with children—even more so when they are very smart. What works with one child may not work with another—even in the same family. And what works with one may not work with that same child in the next situation.

We make our greatest contribution to the education of children when we provide the way for them to develop into lifelong learners. We can then recognize them by the motivations that support their never-ending desire to learn.

Characteristics of Lifelong Learners

1. They **feel free to learn**, to enjoy the excitement and enthusiasm that comes with invention as well as discovery. They experiment and use intuition and imagination as well as logical thinking.

2. They are **dynamic thinkers** who actively engage in trying out their ideas, testing reality, and researching the answers to questions they, themselves, often pose.

3. They **refuse to be pushed into conformity** with rigid patterns, or to bend into compliance with unrealistic expectations.

4. They **reflect a sense of commitment to learning,** to exploring multiple options.

5. They **practice inner self-control** and exhibit self-assurance, high self-esteem, and positive attitudes.

6. They are **flexible** and can adapt the environment and their behaviors to meet changing and unpredictable circumstances.

7. They are **able to match tasks with personal talents,** abilities, and ideals.

8. They **focus** and work on a given task until it is complete.

9. They **reflect** on their own thinking.

10. They possess **wit** and **a sense of humor.**

Prepare for Genuine, Loving Interaction

The interchange with a baby or young child is one of the most exciting experiences an adult can have. There is always something new to see and hear. Since children develop so rapidly, you can almost see them unfolding—like time-lapse photography. What can you do to make way for a genuine, loving interchange? From infants to teenagers, there are three actions adults can take for building relationships.

1. **Watch intently.** See the child as a whole person. Watch a baby's body movements, facial changes, eye movements, hand gestures, finger movements, and mouth and tongue movements. Notice how a child uses distraction to change a situation. Manipulation seems already mastered, as the child can make you change your position or mood. Watch for shifts in behavior of older children, as these may signal a call for help.

2. **Listen receptively.** Hear the child's entire message. Listen for breathing, vocalizations, changes in tones of gurgles, and coos of a baby. Listen for hidden messages by awareness of voice tone, words, and phrases of a young child. Hear the teenager's story

within a story, the humor, the emotion, and the message that comes with silence.

3. **Interpret carefully.** Translate the child's messages. Intuit the meanings that are shared during play or times together. Sense the messages while feeding and changing, holding, or rocking and cuddling the baby. Talk with children, and play back to them what you think they are saying and feeling. Avoid second-guessing or taking a child of any age for granted. Clarify your interpretation, especially with young children and adolescents.

Why Is Adult-Child Interaction So Important?

• **Styles of interacting begin to form early.** Babies develop a style that is unique to each of them as they begin to interact with you and others who care for them. As babies make eye contact, they are making personal connections. Attachment and bonding are strengthened as parents hold and touch their infants and talk with them. By toddlerhood, most parents recognize the unique style of each child.

This is the time in a child's life when patterns are forming for behaving and communicating. Many of these patterns will evolve and change, yet the basis for them begins early.

• **Cycles of engagement are established.** A baby looks at her daddy, and he responds—in turn, the baby responds, and the cycle begins. Moms and babies engage each other differently from dads and babies. A baby is able to know the difference and respond to each in a way that sets up a unique relationship between the two.

Isn't it amazing that parents and caregivers can simply engage themselves with a baby, and the baby takes over? When a baby laughs and squeals with delight, the adult wants to play and interact. But when the baby stiffens and cries, the adult feels like backing away. Babies have lots of control over adults right from the beginning.

One of the overall aims of interacting with children of any age is to make way for them to find their own inborn rhythms. That is, to help them "get in touch" with their own sensitivity to life itself. This gives them a basis for relating to others, who also have their own unique patterns.

Creativity

Smart children are creative thinkers, shaping new ideas and formulating questions sparked by spontaneous wonder. They come up with notions that may be viewed by others as "off the wall." At times, they may appear scattered or fragmented, disregarding the mundane—like keeping an orderly room or tending to household chores.

Creative, in the context of this discussion, is defined as having the power to produce something unique by the application of *divergent*, or different, thinking, whether in verbal, nonverbal, concrete, or abstract form. Imaginative and inventive qualities undergird the creative child's ability to take action in order to develop an idea, produce a composition, or complete a task. The creative child puts a "new twist" on ideas.

We might say the creative child has an *internal locus of perception*. That is, the child is in control of thinking, feeling, and considering possibilities that, in turn, lead to doing something that reflects meaning for the child. The creative child usually feels free to follow natural inclinations without reservations or feelings of obligation as to what someone else might think.

During the first ten years of life, children are naturally inclined toward creativity because the brain favors *spontaneous* thought that emerges with lots of visual and imaginative stimulation. Younger children do in their minds what they cannot do in reality. For example, five-year-old Todd saw a cloud formation and said: "That looks like a spaceship. If I were Superman, I would fly up there and ride through space and zap the garbage with a laser beam and make everything nice." This five-year-old activated his imagination and may actually believe, at some level, that what he said is possible. A nine-year-old, on the other hand, might make a similar statement as a way of expressing concerns and possibilities.

Teenagers use a vast array of metaphors and other figures of speech to express ideas or to get a point across. Printed here with permission is one such list by a fifteen-year-old:

1. "The defenseless essays cried for help as they were being relentlessly attacked by a merciless proofreader." — Personification

2. "Our grades remained conspicuously calm as they were being decapitated without pity." —Personification

3. "The chances of success were as likely as the speed distribution function for a particle with zero velocity." — Simile

4. "The endless cascade of homework assignments was partly responsible for my having received failing grades in nine of my classes." —Metaphor

5. "Our performance here is as essential as 3-b-hydroxysteroid dehydrogenase and 17-a-hydroxylase are to ovarian steroid biosynthesis." —Simile

6. "My test scores are similar in magnitude to the noise level in the dorms after lights-out." —Simile

7. "Sleep became as plentiful as tritium." —Simile

8. "Our refrigerator could not appease the ravenous hunger of the newly arrived Martian." — Personification

9. "Armies of exams were unleashed upon our defenseless minds." —Metaphor

10. "Our semester averages tumbled, screaming, into a bottomless pit." —Personification

—Anonymous, Age 15

Creative children enjoy the excitement that comes with exploring and expressing ideas. They are attracted to the arts, music, and dance because these are ways to actually manifest their feelings and thoughts. Some of the most profound movements—for good or for bad—have been initiated by individuals who created a stir by bringing attention to an issue through unusual music, art, or fashion. Punk rock musicians with outlandish hairdos and clothing are a case in point. So if your teenager dresses in a way that you simply cannot fathom as real, look behind the expression.

Characteristics of Creative Thinkers

Watch children, and listen to them for clues to their creative thinking. You may recognize some of these characteristics:

- **Divergent:** Thinking is self-directed, yet open.
- **Spontaneous:** Thoughts and actions emerge naturally without constraint.
- **Imaginative:** Mental images help formulate ideas and solve problems.
- **Inventive:** Ingenuity evokes new propositions.
- **Enthusiastic:** Energy flows with talents and abilities.

Balancing Creativity and Action

Children are generally driven, or even controlled, by their talents and abilities during the first ten years. They tend to follow their natural inclinations. Children can be found playing musical instruments "by ear," drawing and painting with great intensity, and working for hours building constructions. This is the time to watch out for those young masterminds who take things apart or create messes that change the world forever—or at the time, it seems that way.

Then, around eleven or twelve years of age, children make a turn and take control of their creative abilities. By this time, they seek ways to more formally express themselves, such as by pursuing academic subjects that hold special interest for them. By the time some children are entering junior high, they already know they want to become mathematicians or physicists. Others engage in music lessons and become serious about developing their talents. Still others may be so excited about exploring and learning that creativity actually gets in the way of devoting enough time to all they want to do. Even so, they feel the creative spirit within, and the "call" is usually loud—if not clear.

Fostering a Creative Spirit

Parents and teachers can foster creativity in children by providing environments that entice them to engage in their special interests.

Acknowledge their talents, and they will reflect on their abilities. Give encouragement, and they will continue their efforts. Above all, let them know that you care about them personally, and that their performance or products are simply outcomes and expressions rather than measurements of character. A child needs to know that he or she is valued, regardless of the talents or abilities portrayed.

Focus on children's accomplishments without making moralistic judgments about them. For example, contrast these two statements, and notice how discouraging the first one is compared with the second:

> "What are you doing with all that stuff? I can't imagine that what you are doing is worthwhile."

> "You sure have been working hard on that project. I am pleased to see how much progress you have made—even though I wonder about the mess."

Children who lack self-confidence may hesitate to express themselves, thereby never unleashing their creative potential. We can help by creating an atmosphere that sets children free from perceived notions of ridicule or fear of failure.

The creative child is one who "comes up" with an idea, develops it, and carries it to completion. Children who are free to explore their own ideas and feelings—and then express them—are on their way to creativity. Children who are placed under many restrictions and who must satisfy the expectations of others often are stifled in being creative. Or, they may be creative enough to "get out of" or "away from" the stranglehold they feel is placed upon them. They may even misbehave, run away, or engage in violating the law.

Share time with children, and talk about their interests. Explore their thinking. Ask their advice when issues concern them—and listen intently to what they offer. They may come up with some very divergent, yet possible, solutions.

They also need time alone to daydream and contemplate, to imagine, and to philosophize. Ideas move toward synthesis when one is free to be creative.

Solitude opens the imagination and unleashes creativity.

Super Achievers

Children who are highly motivated to learn and who make outstanding grades in school are often referred to as *super achievers*. Generally, there are two kinds of super achievers. One is the child who has an excellent memory and a high degree of innate intelligence in such domains as math, language, and logic. Another is the child who has a strong drive or high motivation to achieve, whether in music and the arts, or in academics—or both.

Characteristics of Super Achievers
- They usually have a **clear vision of goals** they want to accomplish.
- They are **willing to work hard** to be successful.
- They derive **great pleasure from learning**.
- They are **motivated from within** to pursue knowledge and experiment with their thinking skills.
- They have the ability to **focus on tasks** until they are complete.
- They **see themselves as important** in the eyes of parents, teachers, mentors, and peers.
- They **enjoy positive feedback** and will work hard to get it.
- They **trust in their own abilities** and are **willing to take risks** in order to meet their own expectations.
- They are **sensitive to meeting others' expectations.**
- They generally **accept responsibility** for their own actions.
- They **view success as a natural outcome** rather than a specific goal.

How to Live with a Super Achiever
- **Remember your role as a parent.** Super achievers, as much as any other children, need caring parents. They need lots of support and love. Help them clarify values and participate in family traditions. Establish guidelines for behavior, and enforce limits. Follow through on expectations of your child to assume responsibilities as a family member. These children are eager for recognition from parents for their efforts as well as their accomplishments. They,

like all children, have deep feelings, fears, and disappointments. They count on parents for personal attention to help them cross the hurdles of life.

- **Pick up on clues from their moods and from changes in regular patterns of behavior.** For example, pay attention to a normally outgoing child who becomes especially quiet. Keep the door open for communicating—and for messages of love. Some children worry about school performance, especially taking tests. Even the highest achievers have their moments of doubt.

- **Give the child freedom and responsibility for learning.** Take the child's lead, but watch closely, and listen carefully. Does the child ask a lot of questions? Does the child attempt to take things apart, or explore by getting into things that are off-limits? During the early years, these may be signals that indicate the child is especially bright.

- **Respond by talking with the child or doing things together when you can see this is enhancing the child's efforts.** When a child asks about something, talk about it. If you don't know the answer, then say, "I don't know, but let's find out about this. Let's get out the dictionary or iPad." Or, "Let's get your book and look this up." When a parent says, "That's something you'll have to do in school. I can't help you," the child will likely interpret the message as, *They really don't have the time for or interest in helping me.* Or, the child may think, *I'm not very important.*

- **Avoid intervening when the child is engaged.** Let the child's momentum build from within, from internal motivation. If the child seems a little "weird," so be it. Aren't we all? As long as the child enjoys pursuing the curious and is actively seeking to learn, why get in the way? Roll with the punches, and take the cues from the child. Children who feel free to talk with their parents will do so when the time is right for them. Respond with genuine interest when your child opens the way. Your child will enjoy sharing ideas.

- **Children are "candles to be lit, not bottles to be filled."** Some parents are so eager for their children to achieve success, they try to "pour" information and knowledge into them. Avoid using quizzing and tutoring after school unless a child initiates it. Resist badgering a child to achieve, to work harder and study more. This often turns them off instead of on to studying.

On the other hand, there are parents who feel inadequate to talk with their super achievers, so they tend to avoid issues related to academics. There are also parents who are so preoccupied with the many facets of daily life that they seem never to have time to interact with their children about their pursuits. Take time to let your children know you are interested, even when you don't fully understand what they are doing.

- **Be sensitive to your child's style of motivation.** What is it that seems to drive your child to pursue learning and to work hard? The child who gets excited enough to go further than assignments usually derives great pleasure from learning. One parent offered to do a teenager's chores because she could see that her daughter wanted to rewrite her essay. This kind of support lets a child know that schoolwork is valued in her family.

Some children derive great pleasure from reading. While a child may appear to be somewhat isolated and physically passive, there is a lot of activity going on inside the brain. Reading opens windows to the world. The child who likes to read will gather a great wealth of knowledge and information. Parents can help by allowing the child plenty of time for reading without expectations of spending much time with others.

On the other hand, there are children who need opportunities to talk about what they are doing. Still, others may need time and space to draw pictures, write stories, create poems or songs, draw diagrams, or write essays that express their ideas and interpretations. These children need parents with whom they can share their creations. Parents who respond to these needs by making time and materials available will see the rewards.

- **Make way for your child to have a place to study** and conditions that promote concentration. A child who studies best in a quiet place needs the parent's cooperation to be sure there are no interruptions, such as phone calls, the radio, or the TV. Sometimes even the smartest children need help from parents in establishing sound study habits.

- **Give your child personal recognition for efforts and achievements.** Parents don't have to be as smart as their children to support their efforts. Recognize their work, and let them draw their own conclusions about themselves.

Why Do Smart Children Fail?

While it is true that many smart children fail, it is also true that most of them fail needlessly. Failure is more often a result of a lack of motivation than of a lack of brainpower or intelligence.

Most failures occur for such reasons as:

- Failing to turn in work
- Turning work in late
- Losing assignments
- Failing to ask for help
- Lacking study habits
- Placing little value in academic achievements
- Inadequately preparing for tests
- Lacking concentration on work
- Being preoccupied with too many personal and family problems
- Having an inability to balance emotional stress with school expectations

School Failure Is Personal

Why do so many children have so little desire to achieve in academics? The most likely reason is that children do not grasp the importance of academic success for themselves, personally. They tend to live for the moment, with motivation for immediate satisfaction of personal needs and wants. They do not look ahead several weeks, let alone years, to recognize the value of working hard in school.

These children need to experience the **joy of learning NOW!** That does not mean that schoolwork must be fun. As a matter of fact, most schoolwork is hard work. The joy comes as a result of discovering one's own capacity for thinking, such as grasping the meaning of an idea, a concept, or a new way of solving a problem. Joy is an intensely personal satisfaction that occurs when a person least expects it—often as a result of immersing oneself in a task. The feelings that come with the joy of learning are often enough to motivate a student to study and expand his or her thinking.

Learning becomes desirable for some students when it takes on importance in a social setting. There is a certain element of *social value* that is transmitted within any social setting, whether in families, gangs, or groups of students. By *social value,* I mean that enough people consider it important that others also perceive it as desirable. Examples are certain kinds of music, fashions in clothing, hairstyles, and personal characteristics. Grades and academic standing also can hold social value.

A high school student recently told me that she was jealous of a classmate and friend who was highly respected by her peers. I asked why that was cause for jealousy, and she replied, "Everyone likes me for my social skills, but they respect her for her academic abilities." Then she went on to tell me how she was changing her study habits because she wanted to earn a similar respect. She became motivated by the social value placed on academics by her peers. She wants their respect and is willing to work for it. She is willing to devote more time and energy to studying because she wants recognition that goes beyond friendship.

When we begin to recognize students for their academic efforts and achievements, they will rise to the occasion.

A Philosophy of Caring

The Kind and Gentle Approach

Children of all ages respond positively to the kind and gentle approach. As early as infancy, we see children beginning to reflect caring behaviors. Adults who model kind, gentle, and respectful behavior toward one another provide examples that will influence children and help shape their attitudes about life and the world in which they live. Children surrounded by caring attitudes will become caring individuals.

Adults can be firm and serious, yet kind. They can enforce limits and let children know how far they can go, yet be gentle and warm while interacting.

Children Are Flexible and Resilient

Children by nature have an advantage of being flexible and resilient. They can often "bounce back" from trauma and crises. Many disabilities and disorders can be overcome, or managed, when children experience consistent support and love from parents and other adults who take genuine interest in them.

Perhaps if we believe that every healthy child has limitless intelligence and the capacity to succeed, we will be confident enough to "get out of the way" and let it happen. When we are willing to let the child "carry the ball," we need only stand at the sideline and cheer.

Night and Day's Surprise

Night slowly poured gray soup all over the sky.
She scattered small gems across the sky and left a huge
white smile.
The gems shone like real jewelry.
She let out a breeze, and shot meteors across the sky and
was careful not to sneeze.
Soon Night disappeared, and Day appeared.
Day poured bright colors across the sky, and the gems
disappeared.
She sent the sun out across the bright sky.
The sun was like a huge gem, like Night's small gems.
Soon, she turned the sky to bright blue, and let out a big
breeze.
She made the flowers bloom all across the earth.

—Courtney L. Crawford

Resource Organizations

Parent Support Resources

- Head Start—http://eclkc.ohs.acf.hhs.gov/hslc/HeadStartOffices
    ○ Provides preschool children of low-income families with a comprehensive program to meet their emotional, social, health, nutritional, and psychological needs.
- US Department of Education—http://www2.ed.gov
    ○ Promotes student achievement and preparation for global competitiveness by fostering educational excellence and ensuring equal access.
- Parents as Teachers—http://parentsasteachers.org
    ○ Empowers parents through information, support, and encouragement to help their children develop optimally during the early years of life.

- Eunice Kennedy Shriver National Institute of Child Health and Human Development—http://www.nichd.nih.gov
  - ° Facilitates children reaching their potential overall well-being at all stages of development, as well as mothers achieving good reproductive health through education and rehabilitation.
- The National Center for Family Literacy—http://www.famlit.org
  - ° Inspires and engages families in the pursuit of education through learning together.

Child Development

- The National Association for the Education of Young Children— http://www.naeyc.org
  - ° Serves and acts on behalf of the needs, rights, and well-being of all young children, focusing on the provision of educational, developmental services and resources.
- Centers for Disease Control: Learn the Signs. Act Early—http:// www.cdc.gov/ncbddd/actearly
  - ° Advocates early identification of children with developmental disabilities so children and families can get needed services and support.
- The National Association for Child Development—http://nacd.org
  - ° Provides neurodevelopmental evaluations and individualized programs for children and adults, as well as parent training and parent implementation of the program.
- HealthyChildren.org—http://www.healthychildren.org
  - ° Committed to the attainment of optimal physical, mental, and social health and well-being for all infants, children, adolescents, and young adults through resources provided by the American Academy of Pediatrics.

Children Creatively Endowed

- Autism Society—http://www.autism-society.org
  - ° Provides the most current information and resources for treatment, education, research, and advocacy.

- National Dissemination Center for Children with Disabilities—
  http://nichy.org
  - ○ Provides information, research, and resources to the public
    about issues and topics pertinent to children with disabilities
    (from birth to age twenty-two).

Developmental Expectations

Birth through Prekindergarten

The following developmental expectations are grouped according to levels of development. Each group, from infancy through prekindergarten, is categorized by approximate age spans for reference purposes.

Some of the expectations may overlap from one group to the next, and ages are only approximations because of individual variations. Each child develops at his or her own rate and in a unique way; therefore, these expectations are presented as general guidelines.

Each child progresses from one level to another based on development rather than chronological age. A child has usually achieved most of the expectations by the time a move is made to the next group. Again, these are only guidelines and are helpful in recognizing children's abilities and needs.

These developmental expectations are helpful in knowing what children can do, and for planning activities. They are also helpful in maintaining continuity among what parents, teachers, and caregivers do. Parents and professionals can use these expectations as a common basis for talking about children's progress. The most important consideration is that each child makes progress from one level to another and not in comparison to any other child.

Infants (six weeks to six months)

- Responds to adult's voice, eye contact, and touch, especially that of parents
- Tracks visually by following a moving object or person with eyes and head
- Concentrates focus on adult's face, especially the eyes
- Turns head toward a source of sound
- Plays with own hands and feet
- Lifts head and chest
- Turns over from back to side
- Rotates on tummy with arms, legs, and head lifted (naval rotation)
- Reaches toward objects
- Vocalizes at adult and at own image in a mirror
- Distinguishes mother, father, caregivers (especially by scent, feel, and voice)
- Laughs; babbles; uses series of syllables (ba-ba-ba)
- Imitates mouth and tongue movements of others (facial mimicry)
- Makes anticipatory body movements when wanting to be lifted or held
- Distinguishes between friendly and angry voice tones
- Responds to another infant by reaching, touching, smiling, vocalizing
- Sits alone for a few minutes at a time
- Drops and picks up objects
- Uses arms and legs in unison for push-pull mobility (homologous movements)
- Scoots and moves about two to three feet

- Vocalizes and smiles at strangers and familiar people
- Gets excited by vocalizing and playing when adults, especially parents, approach

Infants (six to twelve months)
- Responds positively to familiar adult voices, eye contact, and touch
- Enjoys touching and manipulating everything (secondary circular reactions)
- Pursues, visually, movements of person and objects
- Holds one object while pursuing another
- Moves toward openings, such as doors, cabinets, and shelves
- Crawls first by using arm and leg on same side (homolateral, crablike)
- Progresses by using right arm and left leg together, then left arm and right leg (contralateral crawl)
- Sits alone easily
- Pulls up by holding onto furniture or person
- Stands and walks with support
- Grasps with thumb and finger (pincer); scoops with hand; holds objects in both hands
- Imitates movements and gestures of others
- Manipulates objects: bangs, throws, rolls, pulls, drops
- Can hold three small objects at a time; puts objects into container
- Holds and manages finger food; feeds self with help
- Begins to hold own bottle; may drink from a cup
- Imitates ritualistic-type play and movements (bye-bye, peekaboo) and some words
- Points to object, and pictures in books while vocalizing
- Knows that a person or object exists even when out of sight; finds objects under a cup, cloth, or furniture (object permanence)
- Uses adult as a helper
- Recognizes familiar in contrast to unfamiliar people; prefers parent or familiar caregiver (has stranger anxiety; may cry or scream when familiar person is replaced by unfamiliar person)

- Responds to adult directions, including "stop" and "no"; is guided by distraction
- Responds to own name

Young Toddlers (twelve to sixteen months)

- Explores parts of toys; probes holes and grooves; pokes object into holes
- Watches moving objects up to ten feet away, including people, animals, vehicles, toys
- Enjoys water play
- Communicates by touching, biting, body language, vocalization with one or two words, short phrases, sound makers
- Enjoys rhythmic movements and sounds
- Drinks from a cup; holds spoon; eats with fingers and spoon; messy; may need some help
- Sits in a chair and eats at a table
- Walks, at first with support; falls easily and bumps head, mouth, and chin; wobbles
- Marks on any surface (paper, walls, furniture) with crayons, chalk, markers
- Looks and grasps objects using forefinger and thumb; releases object with intention
- Climbs up steps on all fours; backs down
- Alternates between crawling and walking
- Controls gross motor movements, such as playing with big balls, push-pull toys, large blocks and cubes, climbing gyms; likes to climb on furniture and into cupboards and various spaces
- Prefers familiar surroundings; small area gives more secure feeling, yet toddler needs to move about freely
- Wants to be independent, yet depends on parents and familiar people (has separation anxiety; may cry or scream when separating from familiar people)
- Uses toys and objects with a purpose in mind (tertiary reactions)
- Discovers own capabilities through trial and error, cause and effect (stacking towers; dropping objects from various heights; pulling, dangling, swinging objects)

- Classifies objects by form, shape, or color (one concept at a time)
- Imitates ritualistic play and movements (enjoys peekaboo, repetitious songs, same stores)
- Enjoys play with parents and familiar people
- Plays alone with objects and toys for several minutes at a time
- Uses position concepts with meaning (up, down, under, on top of, beside, around)
- Discovers new ways to get adults' attention
- Begins imaginative play with dolls, puppets, stuffed toys
- Looks at and responds to own actions (slaps hand and says "no')
- Uses one- and two-word sentences; echolalia (imitates last word or phrase heard)
- Learns sign language easily; understands gestures; makes up body language
- Imitates variety of sounds; "talks" to objects and dolls; imitates mechanical sounds
- Responds to simple adult requests and guidance (receptive language)
- Accepts limits when simple, consistent, and not too many
- Gestures while vocalizing; uses intonation for expression
- Bites to communicate, explore, control, and express anxiety

Toddlers (seventeen months to two years)
- Points to and verbally identifies familiar objects and people in books, pictures, electronic media
- Explores with fingers and gadgets without regard for safety
- Listens to music; makes natural rhythmic movements; likes to dance
- Scribbles with large markers and crayons
- Interested in finger paints, play dough, and tactile materials; attempts to paste
- Enjoys sand, mud, and water play
- Climbs into spaces; runs; jumps
- Improves rapidly in body balance, but still toddles at times
- Begins sphincter control; negotiates corners; still falls
- Catches and throws ball crudely

- Stops and stares during play and when running (gating)
- Eats with spoon; holds cup and glass; sits at table
- Builds tower with cubes; stacks large and small blocks
- Exhibits oppositional behavior; learns to manipulate adults
- Uses toy or object as bridge between self and adult
- Knows purpose of toilet; imitates toileting behavior before ready for training
- Uses mental images to manipulate ideas and wishes (invention of new means: how far to "push" adults, when to change behavior to get wishes, how to use object as toys)
- Remembers relationships, where previous play took place, type of play and toys, who played
- Anticipates; predicts effects by observing; cause and effect is strong
- Pretends, using previous experience and imitation of adult behaviors
- Monologue; "talks" without regard for another's presence; talks simultaneously with others with no regard for the response of others; practices speech; talks to toys and furniture; pretends to read (monologue)
- Sings, alone or with others
- Uses several words; one, two, or three words to express ideas (i.e., "Daddy go bye-bye," "Mommy gone," "go home," "Daddy play")
- Learns sign language easily; uses body language; indicates wants by pointing and using one or two words, or short phrases
- Indicates wet or soiled pants
- Points to familiar objects and people; may call them by name
- Understands and follows simple directions
- Resists limits, yet wants them (feels safe and free to explore within limits)
- Seeks attention by a variety of behaviors: whining, gesturing, tugging, nagging, throwing temper tantrums, charming, etc.
- Uses words or phrases to ask for familiar items, such as milk and cookies
- Increases vocabulary from about twenty to forty words, including the names of people and objects as well as use of verbs

- Enjoys parallel play, alongside others, but not with cooperation; has difficulty sharing
- Strengthens sense self; likes to hear own name
- Forms simple attachments to peers in addition to adults
- Recognizes human and social values transmitted through toys (wants object another child has instead of a similar one on shelf)
- Imitates actions of others
- Plays alone for several minutes at a time
- Depends on parents and familiar adults for emotional support
- Alternates between clinginess and resistance
- Wanders off and returns for eye or body contact with familiar adult
- Carries out two directions
- Explores curiosity about people
- Eats with less help
- Takes off shoes and socks, and sometimes clothes, but needs help getting them on
- Exhibits possessive attitude about toys and parents; may bite; sometimes hits, scratches, pushes to get own way

Younger Two-Year-Olds

Bodily Kinesthetic
- Controls bowels much of the time; ready for toilet training to begin when no longer wobbling, toddling, or stumbling while walking rapidly or running
- Builds tower of four or five large blocks
- Stacks several small table-top blocks
- Goes up and down stairs with one foot leading
- Jumps in place with both feet together
- Pedals tricycle; pushes and steers wheeled toys
- Climbs up and slides down with little or no help
- Runs; jumps; hops; rolls; negotiates turns
- Shows high interest in practicing motor skills
- Scribbles and looks at movements on marking board and paper

- Imitates circular, horizontal, and vertical strokes
- Turns pages in book in single fashion
- Attempts snipping with scissors; cuts gashes in paper with scissors
- Eats with spoon; holds glass easily
- Holds crayon or marker with thumb and fingers
- Opens door by turning handle
- Puts on and takes off jacket; may need help with zippers and snaps
- Washes hands; dries them with help
- Climbs over furniture and structures
- Takes off clothes and socks; may need some help getting them on

Language/Communications
- Recognizes printed name by first letter
- Uses sign language for objects, people, and personal needs
- Recalls animals by picture association
- Points to and names animals and characters in books
- Progresses with speed in vocalizing; has inclinations toward conversations
- Gives attention to language of others, electronic players, TV, radio, telephone
- Understands most simple words and sentences
- Talks to toys, furniture, self, others; listens to self, not others (monologue)
- Talks in short sentences or sentence fragments; varies from three to five words, to six to nine words
- Uses adults, especially parents, as language models

Prelogical/Mathematical
- Develops sense of awareness by involvement with objects, nature, and general surroundings
- Counts randomly without one-to-one relationship
- Plays with small objects and has ability to focus for long periods, depending on interest

- Uses trial and error during play; experiments with variety of materials and objects
- Solves problems during play by using hands, eyes, and body movements
- Concentrates on paths of motion of moving objects
- Perceives and anticipates simple cause-and-effect sequences, chains of events
- Applies nominal realism (the name of an object makes it real)
- Perceives by visual interpretation; if something looks bigger, it has "more" in it (unable to mentally reverse or conserve)
- Classifies according to shape and color (i.e., puzzles, board games)
- Conceptualizes the process of seriation based on actual activities, such as routines, schedules, or familiar activities (first we put on socks, then shoes)

General Thinking/Cognition
- Exercises private logic (magical thinking)
- Thinks that things are alive if they move (animism)
- Decreases staring behavior
- Gains information by looking, listening, and doing
- Learns primarily through play, exploration, and experimentation
- Exercises curiosity and a natural desire to learn about the physical world
- Learns by playing alone and with others
- Exhibits high interest in new situations and new people
- Uses imagination to create reality; may experience new fears (i.e., bathing, sleeping in the dark)
- Imitates and pretends through dramatic play
- Uses role-playing to help understand the real world of family and friends
- Applies prelogical thinking; sees and believes from one's own viewpoint; perception may be incorrect, but is real to the child (preoperational thought)
- Can follow simple directions and limits

Visual Arts/Spatial Ability/Creativity

- Identifies four to eight colors
- Draws and scribbles
- Constructs with blocks and play materials
- Makes collages with paper, cloth, plastic, paste, and a variety of other materials
- Uses finger and brush paints
- Manages to manipulate string, sponge, block painting
- Recognizes own artwork
- Recognizes and names familiar animal pictures
- Recognizes and names self and familiar people in photographs
- Enjoys the process of artwork, using textures, colors, objects, configurations

Music/Movement

- Listens to music, both instrumental and vocal
- Follows simple instructions on musical devices and records
- Uses body movements to express imagination
- Creates rhythmic patterns with musical stimulation
- Responds to repetitious music, poetry, and movements
- Imitates movements of other children and adults
- Likes to dance and use whole body in relation to music
- Attends to classical music
- Sings simple songs, especially with repetitious phrases
- Combines sign and body language with words to create simple songs
- Experiments with simple musical instruments
- Learns words and phrases to familiar songs and tunes
- Recognizes melodies

Personal/Social/Emotional

- Reflects a fairly stabilized sense of self; is somewhat ambivalent about giving up infancy
- Resists and tests limits; oppositional behavior peaks and subsides
- Uses body language to express close ties to mother, father, family, and caregivers

- Begins peer interactions with rising interest in other children
- Pushes and shoves to protect "self-territory"
- Grabs toys to demonstrate sense of "mine"
- Shows greater interest in activities and others outside of home; makes friends with adults
- Begins to control emotions with alternating sudden outbursts and settling
- Clings less to mother; shows more interest in other children and activities
- Attempts to use adult to get wants and needs met
- Resists help from parents and adults; forming greater autonomy
- Reflects growing self-esteem with awareness of self in relation to own name
- Interprets treatment by others as a means of forming self-concept
- Imitates behavior of parents, other adults, and children
- Pushes limits to test reality; wants to know if adults mean what they say

Older Two-Year-Olds

Bodily Kinesthetic
- Walks on line with help of adult
- Jumps in place with both feet while maintaining good balance
- Pedals tricycle with ease
- Negotiates stairs, corners, ducking under, climbing
- Uses slide, swing, outdoor equipment without help
- Copies circle; imitates cross, vertical, horizontal lines
- Traces shapes, including triangle, diamond, circle, square
- Places small pegs in slots
- Laces with cord or yarn in lacing frame
- Uses scissors, paste, paintbrushes, crayons with ease

Language/Communication
- Uses two hundred or more words
- Gives full name on request

- Refers to self by pronoun rather than by name
- Repeats two or three digits
- Names familiar objects (i.e., shoe, coat, crayon, pencil, telephone, etc.)
- Expresses function of some objects (i.e., crayon, ball, book)
- Talks to dolls during dramatic play
- Talks to and around others without regard for their respective responses (collective monologue)
- Practices speech skills in presence of others
- Stutters for several weeks, especially when excited or when thinking faster than speaking
- Facilitates expression with words and body gestures
- Asks questions with "What?" and "Why?" (needs opportunity to learn answer and then respond)
- Uses sign language while talking
- Learns additional languages easily; pronunciation is very accurate
- Enjoys stories; may wander during story, yet continues to listen

Prelogical/Mathematical
- Practices skill of counting without regard for one-to-one or serial relationships
- Counts by rote
- Uses numbers together with hand gestures, such as holding up fingers and saying, "Three."
- Follows numerical request by offering "just one" object
- Ties time concepts to direct experience, such as when to eat, play, sleep (yesterday and tomorrow may be confused; *now* is paramount)
- Learns about time relationships by anticipating routines and activities that are consistent
- Classifies according to concepts of shape, color, size (one concept at a time)
- Seriates with objects of graduated shapes and sizes
- Anticipates consequences of actions, cause-and-effect relationships

General Thinking/Cognition
- Recites letters by rote; sings songs about alphabet
- Recognizes and names some letters
- Recognizes own name, mostly by first letter
- Uses egocentric thinking (time is *now*, place is *here*, center is *me*)
- Lacks ability to use reversibility and conservation concepts
- Imagines and fantasizes; may have fears at night; fear of taking baths is common; may cry or scream when waking from dream
- Learns about roles of parents and others by dramatic play
- Progresses from imitation to modeling by conceptualizing, using memory, and by performance
- Desires to learn through the senses and direct experience; naturally curious
- Masters position concepts (above, below, up, down, beside, under, over, around)

Visual Arts/Spatial Ability/Creativity
- Manipulates paintbrushes, sponges, string painting, finger painting and cloth dipping
- Scribbles, with some drawing attempted
- Positions shapes, cutouts on pages or various surfaces while attempting to paste
- Cuts and tears paper and pastes in own design
- Uses variety of colors and identifies colors by name
- Identifies textures, such as soft, hard, scratchy, rough, slick, smooth
- Follows and copies models with some accuracy
- Enjoys making collages, sculpting, shaping play dough, and painting
- Recognizes own artwork

Music/Movement
- Listens to and follow directions on electronic devices and records
- Imitates animals and characters while listening to records or stories
- Relaxes to classical music

- Anticipates fast and rhythmic musical patterns and combines with body movements
- Balances on toes for a few seconds
- Sings with great interest in repetitious sound effects
- Masters finger plays with singing
- Enjoys songs with repetitious sounds and phrases
- Produces accurate rhythmic patterns to music
- Enjoys using simple musical instruments

Personal/Social/Emotional
- Eats skillfully with spoon
- Pulls clothes off to toilet; may not be able to put on with ease
- Communicates need to toilet; may be able to go with little help
- Imitates toileting process by watching others
- Washes and dries hands, and returns to activity with some help
- Talks in conversational manner during mealtime, yet still in collective monologue style
- Continues to form sense of self, stronger autonomy (personal style becoming evident)
- Takes turns with some continuing difficulty
- Centers on self with egocentric thought still prevailing
- Uses defensive techniques for self-protection, such as telling "untruths" and blaming others
- Uses attention-getting behaviors when seeking adult's attention
- Fears losing prominence when exercising sibling jealousy
- Separates from parent with some difficulty while making transition from toddlerhood to young preschool era
- Reflects ambivalence about independence; may resort to infant-like behavior when under stress, such as with a new baby
- Reflects anxiety of others, especially parents and teachers
- Plays with peers for short periods, mostly parallel play (alongside others, but not with them)
- Forms simple friendships; expresses affection with peers
- Shows affection with adults and siblings
- Approaches adults directly to engage them in play

Younger Three-Year-Olds

Bodily Kinesthetic
- Walks on line in forward position with heel following toe
- Walks on balance beam two to four inches from floor; hops, skips, jumps with ease
- Negotiates stairs, corners; stops and starts with ease
- Masters tricycle and other simple wheeled toys
- Throws ball overhand; catches ball
- Kicks ball with some accuracy, but mostly at random
- Bounces large ball
- Hits volley-type ball with both hands in unison
- Attempts to jump rope
- Builds simple constructions with large blocks
- Manipulates large toys, such as push-trucks, cars, tricycles
- Cuts with scissors
- Traces shapes
- Imitates cross, circle, and triangle with some accuracy
- Places pegs in slots
- Works puzzles with several pieces
- Stacks cubes and table blocks with ease
- Builds constructions with table blocks
- Strings beads with ease
- Manipulates play dough creatively
- Manipulates fine motor materials and toys with skill; copies models with ease

Language/Communication
- Uses simple sentences to express ideas and feelings
- Exhibits capability for broad vocabulary
- Learns new words quickly, especially from adult models
- Practices new words, even out of context
- Gathers information about the world and surroundings
- Continues to use collective monologue (each child talking, but not waiting for responses; several talking at same time)

- Begins having simple conversations, but often resorts to collective monologue (gets carried away with own thoughts)
- Learns second and third languages with ease, especially when practicing at home with parents and siblings, or peers
- Carries out multiple instructions by mastering receptive language
- Listens with interest and imagination to stories being read or told by adults
- Anticipates actions in story with spontaneous comments; recognizes when parts of story are missing
- Follows sequence of story, and recalls characters and story line
- Follows along in book by listening to corresponding sound system
- Makes grammatical errors during speech (i.e., "My mommy *wented* to the store with me.")

Prelogical/Mathematical
- Knows letters of alphabet by rote
- Counts by rote and with some concrete examples can use one-to-one correspondence (i.e., one boy and one dog; two babies)
- Follows instructions that contain a number of objects, such as "Bring two glasses," "Place one paper on the table," or "You may have two cookies."
- Classifies according to shape, color, and size
- Uses seriation with familiar objects, such as lining up objects in order from smallest to largest
- Anticipates consequences, and applies concepts of cause and effect
- Recognizes own name most of the time, especially by first letter
- Prints some numbers and letters when not pushed or pressured
- Forms some shapes and numbers by copying models
- Thinks from own point of view and with own logic ("self" is point of departure—i.e., bigger is better; third place is better because it is a bigger number than first place)
- Makes up rules in order to "win"

General Thinking/Cognition

- Uses own private logic ("If nobody sees me, it's okay for me to eat more cookies.")
- Lacks conservation and reversibility (Changing the shape of a container will automatically change the amount of liquid that is poured into it.)
- Knows primary and secondary colors; learns what happens when primary colors are mixed
- Thinks in egocentric logic (The place is *here*, the time is *now*, and the center of the world is *"ME."*)
- Recognizes some letters on signs, on TV, on containers, and on other objects
- Uses imagination during play and to get "what cannot be achieved in reality"
- Tells "lies" in order to protect self
- Knows roles of parents and other significant adults
- Learns through exploration and pursuing curiosity
- Practices problem-solving skills in practical ways, especially during play
- Knows position and opposition concepts, such as above/below, big/little
- Uses words and language to help control environment and to get attention
- Perceives parents and significant adults as *omnipotent*
- Perceives the world with *animism* (things that move are alive), *artificialism* (the sun is made so we will have light), and *nominal realism* (the name of an object is what it is—we sit on a chair because it is called a chair; trees are tall and shady because they are trees, and we cannot call them something else)
- Learns quickly from models, especially important people, such as parents, family members, and teachers

Makes mistakes as a natural part of learning

- Visual Arts/Spatial Ability/Creativity
- Uses a wide variety of material for artwork (brushes, markers, crayons, clay, finger paints, paste)

- Draws and makes designs on large and small paper or other drawing surfaces
- Draws with chalk on boards and other large surfaces
- Expresses feelings and thoughts through artwork
- Cuts with scissors
- Pastes with glue and other adhesives
- Uses a variety of colors and combines tempera and finger paints to make new colors; likes to experiment with paints and colors
- Identifies textures by feeling the materials
- Copies models with some accuracy
- Enjoys freedom of expression through own creations without models
- Talks about own drawings; can dictate simple ideas or stories for adults to write on child's drawing (brings value to child's work)
- Constructs models with Legos and other construction toys
- Follows design of tracks in games
- Plays games that require following the lines and designs on surface
- Lines up or seriates objects in graduated fashion
- Classifies and groups similar objects and matched designs
- Accomplishes multiple-part puzzles
- Works independently with cognitive and manipulative toys that require spatial relationships

Music/Movement
- Operates simple electronic player or recorder after receiving instructions
- Enjoys variety of music; likes to sing along with recordings and in groups
- Keeps time with simple rhythmic instruments
- Claps to music; marches to music
- Sings with excellent articulation
- Balances on toes, one foot; hops easily; skips
- Controls body motions during musical activities
- Listens to and follows instructions on musical recordings
- Imitates body motions and gestures with musical instruction

- Enjoys repetitious songs and verse; memorizes familiar songs
- Imitates performers, such as peers and media artists
- Relaxes with classical music
- Masters finger plays during singing
- Makes up own movements to music
- Imitates and pretends to be animals and characters
- Concentrates at table activities with baroque background music
- Learns numbers, letters, and directions when set in music fashion; sings numbers and letters

Personal/Social/Emotional
- Reflects sensitivity to what others say; is easily offended; pouts or whines from time to time when things go wrong; feelings are easily hurt
- Communicates needs and wishes with words
- Tattles to adult
- Communicates verbally during play with peers and adults
- Forms friendships easily; may shift spontaneously from one playmate to another
- Makes attachments with several friends; has more than only one special friend, although from time to time chooses to be with only one
- Carries on conversations with adults; can share thoughts or feelings with ease when given modeling by adults
- Understands consequence when explained in simple way by adult
- Wants and needs limits; feels safe with limits; depends on adults to enforce limits
- Pushes limits to test reality of adult in charge
- Uses attention-getting behaviors; still egocentric
- Separates from parent with ease most of the time
- Affectionate with parents, adults, and peers
- Enjoys pets and can learn to care for them
- Likes to please adults and to be a " helper"
- Learns to care for own things with encouragement from adult
- Works out simple social problems with peers; may need some modeling from adults

- Responds to own name; will respond in positive way when name is used with praise and recognition
- Watches adult interactions with other children and generalizes to self
- Can talk things out with adults and peers when guidance is given
- Shows emotion easily; has outbursts of crying; anger is expressed with body and words; sulks when feelings are hurt
- Works to prove independence and autonomy; may push or shove other children; protects own territory and space; still uses such terms as, "It's mine" and, "I can do what I want."

Older Threes and Younger Fours

Bodily Kinesthetic
- Walks on line in forward position
- Balances for five or six seconds on one foot
- Hops in place multiple times
- Jumps over obstacle six to eight inches tall
- Throws ball overhead; catches ball
- Rides wheeled toys with ease
- Copies circles, squares, and other shapes crudely
- Imitates cross
- Traces shapes
- Places small pegs in slots; manipulates fine-motor materials
- Cuts with scissors
- Positions objects; stacks cubes and blocks
- Strings six to eight beads within a few minutes
- Shapes play dough creatively

Language/Communication
- Expresses thoughts and feelings freely with sentences
- Uses broad range of words in vocabulary
- Learns new words easily; practices new words
- Adapts information through speech; attempts to gather facts about "my world"

- Articulates with more conversation and less collective monologue, especially with peers
- Learns additional languages with ease; enjoys sign language
- Carries out three-part instructions by mastery of receptive language
- Listens to story being read or told by adult
- Follows book with corresponding electronic devices
- Enjoys making up stories and songs, and practicing on anyone who will listen

Prelogical/Mathematical
- Concentrates with focus on real objects
- Masters counting skills; uses one-to-one correspondence
- Counts by rote at times; responds to requests for number of items, such as three balls
- Classifies according to shape, color, and size with accuracy
- Seriates familiar objects according to size and visual cues
- Anticipates consequences; uses cause and effect
- Knows most letters of alphabet and can recite them
- Recognizes own name most of the time, still by first letter as cue
- Prints some letters crudely, especially those in own name
- Forms some numbers by copying

General Thinking/Cognition
- Reasons with preoperational thought; cannot conceive of reversibility and conservation
- Uses own private logic
- Considers situations from own point of view
- Knows primary and secondary colors
- Recognizes letters in words, on signs, containers, etc.
- Recognizes own name and names of siblings
- Thinks in very egocentric ways
- Uses imagination and fantasy during play and to "get what I cannot have" in reality
- Knows many roles of adults, especially parents and familiar people

- Learns through exploring and solving simple problems
- Knows *position* and *opposition* concepts

Visual Arts/Spatial Ability/Creativity
- Uses paintbrushes, crayons, markers, and various art materials with ease
- Draws a variety of designs in freehand fashion
- Draws figure of person with head and body, using lines for arms and legs, with few or no details except for some facial features
- Cuts with scissors; likes to cut paper, cotton, cloth, string, other materials
- Pastes with ease; still likes to use lots of paste
- Uses variety of colors; can combine paint to make new color with deliberation (i.e., yellow + blue = green)
- Identifies textures (rough, smooth, soft, slick, etc.) by feeling with hand
- Copies model of line drawing with some success
- Enjoys freedom of expression through own drawings and art designs
- Tells about own drawing
- Builds elaborate constructions with blocks
- Constructs models with Legos
- Follows design of tracks in games
- Imitates body position of others
- Plays games that require following designs on a board game
- Lines up objects in serial order

Music and Movement
- Can operate electronic devices, records, and players
- Enjoys a variety of music
- Likes to dance to a variety of music
- Listens to and follows instruction on records and electronic media
- Follows directions of adult or child in leader role
- Relaxes to classical music
- Is easily stimulated by music

- Claps and marches to rhythmic patterns of music; keeps time with simple rhythmic instruments
- Uses whole body in musical activities
- Sings with excellent articulation
- Sings in solo fashion, especially repetitious verses and tunes
- Imitates performers, such as TV and video personalities
- Imitates patterns of body movements with adult and youth as leader
- Creates patterns with body movement to music
- Memorizes and learns words and songs easily
- Concentrates at table activities with baroque background music
- Masters finger play with ease while singing
- Balances on toes, one foot; hops easily; skips
- Throws and catches ball with hand and arm movements in control
- Kicks ball with accuracy most of the time
- Rolls, tumbles, turns, flips with body; does some cartwheels

Personal/Social/Emotional
- Pouts or whines when feelings are hurt
- Communicates needs and wishes with words
- Tattles to adult
- Communicates with children and adults during play
- Forms friendships easily
- Makes new attachments to one friend at a time
- Eats with skill; uses spoon and fork with ease
- Manages toileting without help; washes hands; returns to activity
- Carries on conversation with adults
- Projects a strong sense of self; autonomy continues to form
- Enjoys sharing most of the time
- Uses attention-getting behaviors often
- Exhibits spurts of separation anxiety when leaving parent (not often)
- Enjoys being leader, or role as big brother or sister
- Shows affection with adults, siblings, and peers
- Enjoys pets and can learn to care for them

- Likes to be the adult's "helper"
- Negotiates with peers by using language; still needs models

Developmental Expectations
Prekindergartners: Older Fours and Younger Fives

Parent Observation Inventory   Date _____

Child's Name _____

The following report is for the period beginning _____
                                    and ending _____ .

This report represents the parent's observations of a child's performance. Fill in the blanks according to the child's ability as observed. This report is designed to estimate a child's progress and is not for use in making school placements or formal evaluations.

The rating scale is based on the following key:

    0 = Never
    1 = Sometimes
    2 = Most of the time
    3 = Always

Developmental Expectations

I. Logic and Math

Builds complex structures with blocks _____

Matches five colors _____

Works seven-_____; nine-_____ piece puzzles

Counts to five_____; ten_____; higher_____

Demonstrates number concepts to five or six _____

Identifies by naming three_____; five_____ shapes _____
Names six basic colors in an activity_____

Matches related objects (fruit; socks; balls)_____

Uses seriation concepts in play (ordering by size) _____

Classifies objects during play _____

Uses cause-and-effect reasoning _____

Knows home address and phone_____

Makes reasonable decision about play _____

Makes choices between alternatives _____

Uses spatial concepts indoors and outdoors _____

II. Language Skills

Receptive
Responds to position concepts
(i.e., "put it in, on, under, beside, etc.") _____

Responds to two-part directions
(i.e., "pass me the ball, and give the bat to me.") _____

Responds to directions involving two objects
(i.e., "Hand me the shoe and the box") _____

Uses body in relation to directions
(i.e., increases pace with "walk fast.") _____

Responds with use of senses
(i.e., "hand me the *soft* ball, *hard* ball, etc.") _____

Comprehension
Knows denominations of coins
(i.e., penny, nickel, dime, quarter)_____

Carries out directions with three parts
(i.e., "pass the bowl, put the shoe on the floor,
and hold the crayon in your hand") _____

Recognizes own name in print or script _____

Responds to own name when spoken to _____

Speech
Names items when asked what is wanted _____

Answers *if, what, when, why* questions
(i.e., "If you had a nickel, what would you do?")_____

Responds to questions about function
(i.e., "What are books for?") _____

Uses sentences with correct grammar_____

Asks *how* questions _____

Uses past and future tense in sentences_____

Uses conjunctions to string words
and phrases together. ("I have a cat and dog") _____

Practices speech with ease when with others
(collective monologue) _____

Engages in meaningful dialogue _____

Uses words and phrases in songs and poems _____

III. Physical and Motor Ability

Large Motor Skills
Negotiates turns and stops; runs at will_____

Balances on one foot for five seconds _____

Hops on one foot; stands on one foot _____

Pushes, pulls, steers wheeled toys _____

Rides and steers tricycle _____

Jumps over fifteen-centimeter-high (six-inch) object
and lands on both feet_____

Throws ball with intentional direction _____

Catches ball bounced to him/her _____

Walks backward: first toe, then heel _____

Marches with cross-lateral arm/leg swing_____

Jumps forward eight times without falling _____

Turns flip (head over heels over head _____

Fine Motor Skills
Builds tower with eight to twelve cubes _____

Drives nails and pegs with hammer _____

Copies circle _____

Imitates cross_____
Cuts on line with scissors _____

Prints a few letters_____

Buckles shoes, buttons clothes, etc._____

IV. Spatial Concepts
Identifies right and left direction
in relation to own body_____

Uses various media to make two-dimensional
representations (e.g., paints, crayons, pens) _____

Uses clay/play dough to make
three-dimensional representations _____

Builds simple constructions with
table blocks _____, building blocks _____

Builds complex structures with table blocks_____
large building blocks_____

Controls body in positions, such as in games
(e.g., freeze, "may I")_____

Negotiates ladders, steps, slides, etc. _____

Knows parts of building (doors, rafters, etc.) _____

V. Music, Art, and Drama

Music
Knows phrases of songs and can sing _____

Listens to short, simple stories (five minutes)_____
Recites nursery rhymes _____

Sings simple songs_____

Enjoys listening to variety of music
(i.e., classical, popular, children's) _____

Shows rhythmic movements with body _____

Recognizes tunes, stories and recites_____

Art
Paints and names own picture_____

Uses several media for two-dimensional
representations (brush, paint, finger paint, felt marker,
crayons, sponge, etc.) _____

Draws head and one___, two___, three___, other____
parts of body on figure _____ _

Manipulates clay and play dough-type substances
(i.e., shaping, designing, etc.) _____

Enjoys using a variety of art materials
(i.e., glue, paper, cloth, wood, etc.) _____

Drama
Imitates character through role-playing _____

Models people (family members, teacher, others)
during play and dress-up_____

Knows roles of family members
through pretend play_____

Engages in creative movements to music _____

Uses imagination during dramatic play _____

VI. Personal Competencies

Self-Awareness
Reflects positive self-image _____

Enjoys doing things alone as well as with others_____

Conversations reflect high self-esteem _____

Makes positive comments about self
(i.e., "I am four years old," "I am big," etc.) _____

Can follow through with decisions
about play and other activities _____ _

Requires minimal amount of attention
beyond normal responses
(i.e., does not have to act out to get attention) __ _____

Aware of self as reflected in behaviors_____

Responsible for own behavior_____

Getting Along with Others

Joins in play with others _____

Shares and takes turns_____ _

Enjoys pretend play, role-playing _____

Interacts with peers, showing respect _____

Follows direction of adults _____

Reflects ability to converse with adults _____

Uses adult as a resource _____

Uses social skills for such tasks as
manners and greeting visitors _____

Shows sensitivity to feelings of others_____

The purpose of this inventory is not to determine a high or low score, but to determine a child's progress in each category. Some children will score higher in some areas and lower in others. This is not a test, but a way for parents to become aware of each child's strengths and interests at the prekindergarten level.

©2013, Wanda Draper, PhD

Recipes for Art Supplies

Basic Art Supplies: For Younger Children

Cooked Play Dough

INGREDIENTS:

- 1 cup all-purpose flour
- ½ cup table salt
- 1 tablespoon oil
- 1 teaspoon cream of tartar
- 1 cup water
- Food coloring (optional)

METHOD:

Mix together all ingredients in a saucepan. Cook mixture over low heat until thickened, stirring constantly. Allow it to cool before using. Store in airtight container when not in use.

Note: This cooked play dough is a better quality than the uncooked play dough. If children happen to eat some, it will be salty, but will not hurt them.

Uncooked Play Dough

INGREDIENTS:

- 1 cup all-purpose flour
- ½ cup salt
- 1 teaspoon oil
- 1 teaspoon cream of tartar
- Food coloring
- Enough water to make dough good handling consistency

METHOD:

Mix all ingredients together except the water. Add the water slowly in small amounts until dough is easy to handle. Store in airtight container when not in use.

Note: Children enjoy helping make this type of play dough.

Putty

INGREDIENTS:

- White glue
- Liquid starch

METHOD:

Mix equal parts of Elmer's glue and liquid starch for a few minutes until smooth. Do **NOT** cook. Store in airtight container.

Goop Dough

INGREDIENTS:

- 1 cup cornstarch
- 2 cups salt
- $^2/_3$ cup water
- ½ cup water
- Food coloring (optional)

METHOD:

Mix 2 cups salt and $^2/_3$ cup water in a small pan and heat over low heat for three to four minutes. Remove from heat. Mix in a separate container 1 cup cornstarch and ½ cup tap water. Blend well. Add cornstarch mixture quickly to the hot saltwater mixture, stirring constantly. This mixture should form a stiff dough. If it fails to thicken, return to heat. Stir constantly.

Mixture may be colored with food coloring. Store mixture in airtight container when not in use.

Creative Ideas:

- Stiff dough lends to modeling objects, which may be painted, dried, and coated with clear lacquer.
- Children enjoy goop dough for modeling objects to decorate their space, or making ornaments for holidays.

Finger Paint #1

INGREDIENTS:

- 1 cup liquid starch
- 6 cups lukewarm water
- ½ cup soap flakes*
- Desired color pigments

METHOD:

Mix the starch into the soap flakes. Gradually add the lukewarm water to the soap-starch mixture, stirring until smooth. Pour into small individual containers. Add pigment to each container of finger paint mixture.

Soap Flakes:

While it is possible to buy soap flakes from online suppliers or markets, the flakes are easily made at home.

Grate your choice of soap (a color-free and irritant-free soap is best, such as a vegetable oil- or glycerin-based soap) with a kitchen grater. Store unused flakes in an airtight container for other uses. Soap flakes also are used as part of eco-friendly and nontoxic cleaning solutions. In addition, there are other arts and crafts possibilities.

Finger Paint #2

INGREDIENTS:
- ½ cup laundry starch
- 1 cup cold water
- 1 quart water
- 1 cup soap flakes
- Desired tempera paint color or food coloring

METHOD:

Dissolve starch into one cup cold water in a pan. Add one quart cold water to this mixture. Place over low heat. Cook until thick, stirring constantly. Remove from heat. Add soap flakes. Stir until well-blended. Add tempera paint or food coloring to mixture. Let cool. Store in a covered container.

Finger Paint Variations

- 1 cup salt may be added to finger paint mixture, as children enjoy the different touch sensation.
- 1 cup sawdust may be added to above recipes, making a consistency of soft putty. This can be shaped, dried, and painted. Then shellac.

Homemade Paste

INGREDIENTS:
- 1 cup sugar
- 1 cup flour
- 1 teaspoon alum
- 1 quart water
- Oil of cloves

METHOD:

Mix all dry ingredients together in a pot. Add water. Cook until it is thick, stirring constantly. Cool. Add several drops oil of cloves. Store in covered jars.

Flour Paste

INGREDIENTS:

- ½ cup flour
- Water
- Wintergreen or peppermint oil

METHOD:

Add enough water to make a thick paste. Boil five minutes over medium heat, stirring constantly. Cool and thin with water. Add a few drops wintergreen or peppermint to keep it from spoiling. Keep in a covered jar. Use in any projects requiring large quantities of paste.

Cornstarch Paste

INGREDIENTS:

- 2 tablespoons cornstarch
- Water

METHOD:

In a pot, add enough cold water to the cornstarch to make a smooth paste. Gradually and slowly, add boiling water until the mixture turns clear. Cook until it thickens, and remove from the heat. This paste becomes thicker as it cools. It may be thinned with water.

Use Note:

Use cornstarch paste on tissue paper or thin cloth, since it is less likely to show through than flour paste.

Powder Paint #1

INGREDIENTS:

- 5 tablespoons powder tempera paint
- 5 tablespoons water
- Liquid starch or detergent (optional)

METHOD:

Put powder paint and water in an empty milk carton or other container. Press the lid down firmly, and shake the carton until the paint is thoroughly mixed. To make the paint keep better and go on more smoothly, add enough liquid starch or detergent to make it the consistency of cream.

Powder Paint #2

INGREDIENTS:
- 8 tablespoons powder tempera paint
- 1 teaspoon white library paste
- 2 tablespoons liquid starch

Oil of cloves, wintergreen, or peppermint (optional)

METHOD:

Add enough water to give the mixture a consistency of cream. To prevent a sour smell, add a little oil of cloves, wintergreen, or peppermint.

Powder Paint Watercolors

INGREDIENTS:
- For transparent watercolor
  - ° Powder paint
  - ° Water
- For opaque watercolor
  - ° Powder paint
  - ° Liquid starch and small amount of water

METHOD:

Transparent watercolor: Add sufficient water to the powder paint to obtain a runny consistency.

Opaque watercolor: Add enough water or liquid starch to the powder paint to make a creamy consistency.

Paint Pointers

MIXING COLORS:
1. For bright powder paint, add a small amount of glycerin or evaporated milk to make the powder paint glossy.
2. Darker colors can be made by adding black, blue, brown, or purple to the color mixture.

3. For pastel colors, start with white, and gradually add more color until the desired tint is reached. This will save paint. For example, white with a small amount of red added will give a tint of pink.

4. Red, orange, and violet are difficult pigments to mix with water. A few drops of alcohol will speed the mixing.

5. Buttermilk paint: Use buttermilk instead of water when mixing powder tempera paint. The result will be a chalklike effect, which will not rub off.

Paint Saver

INGREDIENTS:

- 2 tablespoons powder tempera paint
- ½ cup powdered laundry detergent

METHOD:

Put powder paint and detergent in an empty milk carton or jar. Cover firmly, and shake until the paint is thoroughly mixed. Add water to make consistency for spreading with paintbrush. (Spills wash out of clothes easily!)

Advanced Art Supplies: For Older Children

Oil Paint

INGREDIENTS:

- Glycerin
- Powder tempera
- Raw linseed oil

METHOD:

Add a few drops of glycerin and desired powder tempera color to raw linseed oil. Add enough to make a thick, creamy consistency.

Enamel Paint

INGREDIENTS:

- Clear shellac or varnish
- Powder tempera

METHOD:

Add clear shellac or varnish to the powder tempera paint until a desired brushing consistency is reached.

Wood Stain #1

INGREDIENTS:

- Powder tempera
- Turpentine or liquid starch
- Varnish

METHOD:

Mix 2 tablespoons powder tempera paint with turpentine or liquid starch to make a thick paste. Add varnish until mixture is smooth.

Wood Stain #2

INGREDIENTS:

- Crayons
- Wood project
- Linseed oil

METHOD:

Rub crayons on the wood, going with the grain. Then, rub the wood vigorously with a cloth saturated in linseed oil.

References

American Psychiatric Association: Diagnostic and Statistical Manual of Mental Disorders, Fifth Edition. Arlington, VA: American Psychiatric Association, 2013.

Brazelton, T. Berry and Stanley I. Greenspan. *The Irreducible Needs of Children: What Every Child Must Have to Grow, Learn, Flourish.* Massachusetts: Da Capo Press, 2009.

Buzan, Tony. *The Ultimate Book of Mind Maps.* London: Thornson, 2005.

Buzan, Tony. *Use Your Head.* London: BBC Active, 2006.

Fonagy, Peter. *Attachment Theory and Psychoanalysis.* New York: Other Press, 2001.

Gardner, Howard. *Frames of Mind: The Theory of Multiple Intelligences.* New York: Basic Books, 1983; 2011.

Gardner, Howard. *Multiple Intelligences: New Horizons in Theory and Practice.* New York: Basic Books, 2006.

Gruber, Howard E. and J. Jacques Vonèche, Eds., *The Essential Piaget: An Interpretive Reference and Guide.* New York: Basic Books, 1995.

Perry, Bruce D. and Maria Szalavitz. *Born for Love: Why Empathy Is Essential—and Endangered.* New York: HarperCollins, 2010.

Restak, Richard M. *Think Smart: A Neuroscientist's Prescription for Improving Your Brain's Performance.* New York: Riverhead Books, 2009.

Sinetar, Marsha. *Do What You Love, The Money Will Follow: Discovering Your Right Livelihood.* New York: Dell Publishing, 2011.

Stern, Daniel N. *The First Relationship: Infant and Mother.* Cambridge: Harvard University Press, 2002.

Index